The $100,000+
Job Interview

WENDY S. ENELOW, CCM, MRW, JCTC, CPRW

IMPACT PUBLICATIONS
MANASSAS PARK, VIRGINIA

ISBN: 1-57023-222-9

Library of Congress: 2004110019

Publisher: For information on Impact Publications, including current and forthcoming publications, authors, press kits, online bookstore, and submission requirements, visit the left navigation bar on the front page of our main company website: www.impactpublications.com.

Publicity/Rights: For information on publicity, author interviews, and subsidiary rights, contact the Media Relations Department: Tel. 703-361-7300, Fax 703-335-9486, or email: info@impactpublications.com.

Sales/Distribution: All bookstore sales are handled through Impact's trade distributor: National Book Network, 15200 NBN Way, Blue Ridge Summit, PA 17214, Tel. 1-800-462-6420. All special sales and distribution inquiries should be directed to the publisher: Sales Department, IMPACT PUBLICA-TIONS, 9104 Manassas Drive, Suite N, Manassas Park, VA 20111-5211, Tel. 703-361-7300, Fax 703-335-9486, or email: info@impactpublications.com.

Contents

Preface

I N DECADES GONE BY, "job search" was usually a breeze. You mentioned to a few people that you were "in the market" and before you knew it, people were calling and offering you opportunities. It was a great life!

Now, compare that to today's job search market where hundreds of candidates are often vying for the same position. You're dealing with an entirely different situation where you have one, and only one, opportunity to make an impression – your job interview. As such, it is critical that you be a competent and savvy job seeker who knows "how" to interview, "what" to say, and "when" to say it.

Once you've read this book, you'll be equipped with the strategies, knowledge, and techniques that will strengthen your interviewing skills, sharpen your ability to "think on your feet," and propel you to the top of the list of qualified candidates. Learn what the experts have to say about how to make a lasting impression and win that all-important job offer!

1

Welcome to the World of Interviewing

I T'S 9:15 A.M. AND YOU'VE been sitting in the reception area for 20 minutes now, waiting for them to call you. You're nervous. This is a big interview, the biggest of your life. The opportunity is ideal for you. With more than 15 years' experience as Treasurer/CFO of both a hardware manufacturing company and a dotcom venture, you're now poised to take the helm as President/CEO of this Fortune 500 company. You know the competition is fierce, yet you've already made it to round #4 in the interview process. You know they are considering only three other candidates at this point and you feel reasonably confident.

But this is your last chance. You know that today – in front of the entire Executive Committee and Board of Directors – you must impress them or you'll never get back in the door again. This is it. Even though you know you are extremely well qualified and would excel in the position, you are apprehensive. On the outside, you're calm and collected; on the inside, your heart is beating fast, your pulse is racing, and your mind is going a million miles a second. There is so much you want to be sure to communicate. Can you remember it all? Will you present yourself well? Can you demonstrate that you really can be a valuable asset to the management team, the board, and the company?

Just then the receptionist walks up and asks you to follow. Slowly, you both make your way down two long corridors and walk into a brightly lit conference room. There are 12 of them – eight men and four women – all eyeing you as you walk in, greet them each individually, and take your seat. What tremendous power and control these 12 people hold today – people who are probably no more qualified nor more successful than you. Your destiny is in their hands.

Play to Win!

Do those 12 people really have all of the control? To some degree, yes. Ultimately, these 12 individuals will make a hiring decision that will, in the short term, significantly impact your career and perhaps your self-esteem. You know you are qualified, you know you can perform well beyond their expectations, and you know that you can deliver strong results. Today's most significant challenge is to build rapport and trust, and to begin to immerse yourself into the company's culture and its inner circle.

But you have power too. What transpires in that conference room is largely up to you. Will you be in control of the interview? Will you be effective in communicating information regarding your professional experience, skills, achievements, and personal attributes that is so critical to demonstrating your value to the company and distinguishing yourself from the other candidates? Will you be able to start to build the relationships today that will be vital to your selection and your ultimate success?

Yes, you can. If you are an educated job seeker with strong interviewing skills, you already know that you have the control and the power to shape your own destiny. You walked into that conference room with your own personal agenda – information to communicate, skills to demonstrate, problem-solving competencies to highlight, and successes that validate it all. Your goal is to keep the interview heading in a positive direction, providing you with the opportunity to communicate what is most important. You must keep your mind focused, your senses alert, and your responses to their questions right on target. Your physical appearance and demeanor must be sharp; you must communicate your high level of personal integrity and ethics. It's all up to you. Are you ready for the challenge? Can you win at the interviewing game?

Powerful Performance

For many individuals this type of interview situation can be extremely intimidating. It's not just you and the human resources manager sitting comfortably in a private office discussing your past experiences and interest in the company. It's not just you and the retiring treasurer exploring the specific job responsibilities. It's not just you and the CEO chatting about the company's needs, vision and long-term objectives. These situations would be much more comfortable, easier to manage, and less threatening. Rather, it is a situation where 12 top executives are scrutinizing you, listening to every word you say, and watching every move you make. Why wouldn't you be a bit intimidated and nervous? The rest of us certainly would be!

The stress you feel in this interview or any other type of interview situation is not only normal, it's useful. The adrenaline flowing through your body makes you sharper, more alert, and more focused. One of the world's most renowned opera singers has said that after more than 20 years on the stage, as she waits behind the curtain before each performance, she feels the stress, the nervousness, and the adrenaline. It is this energy that excites her and pushes her to perform. The same can be said about interviewing. If you can harness the energy and push it in a positive direction, it will give you power.

> *Stress can be a positive reaction to interviewing, for if you can channel that energy in the right direction, it will give you the "power to perform."*

Think of your interview just like that – a platform on which to perform. You're in the spotlight and you've got a script (AKA agenda) to communicate to your audience. The energy rushing through your body is simply stage fright that, when harnessed, will give you the strength, the intensity, and the power to win over your audience.

Interview Success Strategies:
The Candidate

When you enter an interview situation, you must be prepared with your own agenda – critical messages you wish to communicate to your interviewer. For the executive job seeker, these must include the following, which are easy to remember since, if you use the first letter of each word, they spell the word "interview":

Integrity

Negotiate

Trust

Enthusiasm

Rapport

Vitality

Innovation

Educated

Win

Integrity   The thought may be trite, but people want to hire people who are honorable, ethical, and have a high level of personal integrity. When you are employed by an organization, particularly in a senior-executive position, you represent the company in everything that you do. In any interview, your #1 objective is to communicate that you operate at the highest level of personal and professional standards. Let your interview(ers) and the company know that they can trust in your integrity, your performance, and your word.

Negotiate   Your ability to negotiate will be critical throughout the entire interview process. Not only will you be negotiating your salary, bonus structure, benefits, and total compensation package (see Chapter 6), you will be negotiating for an opportunity. Look at interviewing as a unique negotiation between two parties working to achieve consensus. Your objective is to bring the interviewer over to your "side of the table" and win the job offer.

Trust   Building trust with your interviewer is critical. To be embraced by a company, there must be an immediate sense of trust between all parties. Be honest and above board with all of your answers, working hard to position them positively, but remaining truthful. If, for whatever reason, you are not able to build a sense of trust, chances are your first interview will not result in a second interview or an offer.

Enthusiasm No one wants to hire someone who is lackadaisical, unmotivated, and "just there." Your challenge in any interview situation is to demonstrate your enthusiasm – for the position, for the company, and for the opportunity. Enter the interview with excitement, a smile on your face, and a spring in your step. Do this and the entire atmosphere will be energized. You feel it and so will your interviewer, leaving a long-lasting and positive impression.

Rapport Building rapport with your interviewer is vital. No interviewer is going to recommend a second interview or make an employment offer to an individual whom he feels uncomfortable with. Be sure that one of the most important items on your interview agenda is developing rapport with your interviewer.

Vitality Demonstrate a sense of energy, drive, and enthusiasm every step of the way in the interview process. Companies want to hire individuals who are vital, dynamic, self-motivated, and driven to succeed. Be sure that you have communicated that message. This is particularly true for older candidates who must – right or wrong – demonstrate that they are energetic, youthful, and competent; not "over-the-hill" executives.

Innovation The employment market is more competitive than ever before. To give yourself a competitive edge over other candidates, you must demonstrate your innovation. This can include specific achievements, project highlights, processes you have redesigned and improved, problems you have solved, new products you have developed, new revenue streams you have created, and your specific contributions to bottom-line profitability. Utilize your career success to demonstrate innovation and results.

Educated Communicate that fact that you are well educated, either through formal training and/or life experiences. Companies want to hire individuals who are well-versed in their chosen profession and industry. Demonstrate your knowledge through your resume, your conversation, and your ease in presentation style. If you have attended professional training and executive development programs, share that information. If you have led nonprofit organizations, spoken at national conferences, written for trade publications, and the like, share that information. All of this serves to further validate your qualifications and your credibility beyond "just" your full-time professional work experience.

Win Bottom line, in any interview situation, your objective is to win – win the next interview, win the support of your interviewer, and, ultimately, win the opportunity. Interviewing can be a stressful situation, fraught with pitfalls to exclude you from consideration. Consider it one of life's most challenging games. Your goal is to win against the competition and get the offer, even if you do not ultimately accept the position. Never let this thought leave you.

Interview Success Strategies:
The Interviewer

When an HR executive, hiring manager, or other individuals interview you, they have their own agenda – part personal and part on behalf of the company. Not only must you stick with your own agenda, you must be responsive to theirs. Again, these are easy to remember since they spell the word "interview":

> Investigate
> Notice
> Transcend
> Exclude
> Research
> Validate
> Interrogate
> Extrapolate
> Wise Decisions

Investigate   The interviewer's #1 objective is to "investigate" who you are, the qualifications you bring to the company, your level of professional competency, and other information relevant to the particular opportunity at hand. Interviewing is truly an exploration and discovery process, allowing your interviewer to uncover the obvious and the not-so-obvious facts.

Notice   An interviewer's challenge is to notice everything about you, that which is readily apparent and that which is not. It may be your ability to make and retain eye contact, your firm handshake, your style of dress, your personal hygiene, the length of your hair, how you sit, how you walk, where your hands are when you stand, your handwriting, and so much more. The interviewer takes mental notes throughout the process and then documents all of this information. Your challenge is to physically present yourself as an executive – from the suit that you are wearing to the manner in which you stand and meet others.

Transcend　One of the greatest challenges facing every interviewer is his ability to transcend what you are saying to get to the real message. Here's an example. Suppose the interviewer inquires about your experience in personnel training, development, and direct supervision. The reality may be that you have none, but you certainly don't want to communicate that message. Instead, you might say, "Throughout my career, I have always worked with cross-functional, cross-departmental project teams. My role has been to coordinate project assignments, scheduling, reporting, and administration for groups of up to 35 personnel. This has been particularly challenging in our environment where there has been a tremendous hiring influx and the need for ongoing job training and support." If the interviewer is able to effectively transcend, he/she will realize that what you've really said is "No."

Exclude　One of the primary objectives of an interviewer (particularly in phase #1 of the interview process) is to exclude potential candidates and the number of individuals moving to phase #2. Feel comfort in the fact that if the interviewer or company did not believe that you had the basic qualifications, you would not have even been invited for interview #1. So, remind yourself, when you get nervous, that you're already passed the preliminary screening and approach the interview confident in your abilities. However, if, after this stage, you are excluded for whatever reason, let it go. All too often job seekers work to recapture an opportunity that, for whatever reason, has been lost. If the interviewer does not believe you to be an appropriate candidate, it is extremely unlikely that you can change her mind no matter what you say or do.

Research   Be advised that the interviewer and/or the company will closely research your background – whatever they can find out and from whomever. Of course, at some point, they will contact your references, but many companies go well beyond basic reference checking. Remember, the higher the level of position, the closer the scrutiny. Can you withstand this type of research into your background – personal and professional?

Validate   At some point in the process, the interviewer (or someone else within the company) will be responsible for validating the information you have presented in your resume and during the interview. Be sure that you have been 100% honest and accurate in your presentation of ALL the facts – employment history, position titles, dates, educational qualifications, technical skills, project highlights, quantifiable results, and more. If, during the company's background check, they are unable to validate the information that you have provided, you have lost and can never recapture the opportunity.

Interrogate   Although this may seem a bit harsh, an inter-viewer's goal is to interrogate, questioning you, your skills, experiences, competencies, achievements, successes, project highlights, and more. The task at hand is for them to delve as deeply as possible into your career history to explore all of the qualifications, skills, experience, and more you bring to that position. Do not be threatened, but, rather, view the interrogation as an opportunity.

Extrapolate   Any qualified interviewer comes to each interview with a specific agenda regarding information that he wants from you relative to your skills, experiences, and competencies. He will have developed targeted questions and points of conversation to extrapolate that specific information. Be advised that you always want to answer each and every question in full, but you also want to be certain that you address your own agenda of information you believe is important to communicate in this particular interview.

Wise
Decisions   Ultimately, at any stage in the executive-interview process, the interviewer is challenged to make wise decisions. Should this candidate be excluded for any particular reason? Should this candidate be invited back for another interview, further up in the chain of command? Should we make an offer to this candidate? What are the risks involved in hiring this individual? What are the potential rewards in hiring this candidate? Provide your interviewer with solid information, verifiable results, and a strong track record of performance, and you will strengthen her decision-making ability. Remember, a key indicator of interview success is the relationship you build with the interviewer and what reflection that will have on your interviewer should she make you an offer. She's putting her reputation on the line by selecting you as

someone who will bring value, deliver results, and perform as expected. In turn, she is intensely motivated to make a wise hire.

Power Words for Interview Success

The following three lists of power words and phrases will allow you to create a sense of energy, excitement and success in your interviews. Use these key words as appropriate to communicate your skills, qualifications, achievements, and track record of performance. Do not simply throw them into the conversation, but, rather, use them to highlight specific positions, responsibilities, projects, challenges, and accomplishments.

Executive Skill Sets

Review the following list carefully and highlight the items that match your skills, career history, and achievements. Then integrate them as appropriate into your interviews. Note that many of these skills are key qualifications for virtually every executive position.

- ❑ Benchmarking and Best-in-Class Practices
- ❑ Board Relations and Presentations
- ❑ Business Planning
- ❑ Change Management
- ❑ Competitive Negotiations and Wins
- ❑ Corporate, Customer, and Employee Communications
- ❑ Cost Reduction and Avoidance
- ❑ Customer Service, Retention, and Loyalty
- ❑ Efficiency Improvement
- ❑ Executive Leadership
- ❑ Fast-Track Promotion
- ❑ Financial Control
- ❑ Financial Leadership

- ❑ Global Expansion and Diversification
- ❑ High-Growth Organizations
- ❑ International Business Affairs
- ❑ Joint Ventures, Partnerships, and Strategic Alliances
- ❑ Market Expansion and Diversification
- ❑ Market Image and Perception
- ❑ Market Share Increases
- ❑ Mergers and Acquisitions
- ❑ Multinational Organizations
- ❑ New Venture Development and Launch
- ❑ Organizational Development and Leadership
- ❑ PC and Internet Proficiency
- ❑ Performance Improvement & Management
- ❑ Process Redesign and Simplification
- ❑ Product Design, Development, and Commercialization
- ❑ Productivity Improvement
- ❑ Profit and Loss Management
- ❑ Profit and Revenue Improvement
- ❑ Quality Improvement
- ❑ Relationship Building and Management
- ❑ ROA, ROE, and ROI Gains
- ❑ Shareholder and Stakeholder Value
- ❑ Start-Up Enterprises and Ventures
- ❑ Strategic Planning and Vision
- ❑ Success and Results
- ❑ Total Quality Management
- ❑ Transition Management
- ❑ Turnaround and Revitalization
- ❑ World Class Operations

Personal and Professional Characteristics

Review the following list carefully and highlight the items that match your personal and professional characteristics. Then integrate them

as appropriate into your interviews. Note that many of these characteristics are vital to every executive hire.

Accomplished	Dedicated
Adaptable	Dependable
Analytical	Determined
Assertive	Devoted
Authentic	Diligent
Believable	Diplomatic
Bold	Direct
Charismatic	Dynamic
Competent	Earnest
Competitive	Effective
Conceptual	Efficient
Confident	Eloquent
Conscientious	Encouraging
Courageous	Energized
Creative	Enterprising
Credible	Enthusiastic
Customer-Driven	Entrepreneurial
Decisive	Ethical
Expressive	Practical
Flexible	Pragmatic
Honest	Precise
Honorable	Prepared
Humanitarian	Productive
Imaginative	Proud
Independent	Prudent
Industrious	Reputable
Ingenious	Resilient
Insightful	Resourceful
Intelligent	Responsive
Intense	Savvy

Intuitive	Sharp
Loyal	Sophisticated
Market-Driven	Stalwart
Mature	Strategic
Methodical	Strong
Motivated	Subjective
Multilingual	Successful
Nurturing	Supportive
Objective	Tactful
Observant	Tactical
Organized	Talented
Perceptive	Tenacious
Perservering	Thorough
Persistent	Tolerant
Personable	Trustworthy
Persuasive	Vigorous
Poised	Visionary
Polished	Vital
Positive	Wise

Personality and Style Descriptors

Review the following list carefully and highlight the items that best describe your personality and style. Then integrate them as appropriate into your interviews. Note that many of these characteristics are essential for powerful executive performance.

Advocate	Leader
Catalyst	Listener
Champion	Manager
Coach	Mediator
Confidante	Mentor
Consensus Builder	Negotiator
Decision Maker	Pioneer

Delegator	Problem Solver
Driver	Team Builder
Influencer	Troubleshooter
Innovator	Winner

About This Book

This book has been written to carefully guide you through the interview process by giving you the tools and knowledge you need in order to succeed – no matter the type of interview you may encounter.

Chapter 2 focuses on the critical importance of interview preparation and what you can do to fully equip yourself to succeed.

Chapter 3 details the various types of interviews – traditional, situational, and behavioral – as well as the different interview situations – informational, networking, phone screening, electronic screening, hiring, and more.

Chapter 4, one of the most critical in this book, addresses how to overcome interview challenges that you may encounter if you've been fired from your last position, if you're considered over-qualified, if your recommendations are poor, and more.

Chapter 5 explores how to answer specific interview questions by providing you with scripted answers that you can edit for your own use and presentation.

Chapter 6 talks about money (a subject that's always at the heart of any interview) and outlines effective strategies for negotiating favorable compensation packages.

Chapter 7 focuses on follow-up and its critical impact on how well you and your candidacy are reviewed.

Chapter 8 offers you proven strategies, tips, and techniques from hiring managers, recruiters, outplacement consultants, resume writers, career coaches, and career counselors – all valuable information in obtaining an interview and winning an offer.

Chapter 9, the final chapter in this book, will hopefully provide you with the motivation, insight, and expertise to nail each and every one of your interviews.

2

Prepare to Win!

P REPARING FOR YOUR JOB SEARCH and winning a
new opportunity involves a complex, multi-tiered process where you must:

1. Clearly define your objective(s), taking advantage of the
vast number of online assessment tools that are now
available to be sure you're clearly focused and satisfied
with your career direction.

2. Develop powerful career marketing communications (e.g., re-sume, cover letter, career portfolio, leadership profile).

3. Determine which career marketing activities (e.g., ad responses; networking; online job and resume postings; targeted email campaigns to companies, recruiters, and/or venture capital firms; job fairs) are appropriate for your search and will most likely uncover the right opportunities.

4. Develop your marketing plan and effectively manage its implementation.

All of those activities come before you actually begin to interview. In fact, those activities are vitally important to your successful search, and you must spend the appropriate time and energy to clearly define your career path, create an outstanding resume, and launch a campaign that will place you (your resume) in front of the audiences that would be most interested in a candidate with your qualifications. There are hundreds of books written on these topics; two of mine that will be of the most help to you are:

- *Best Resumes For $100,000+ Jobs* (Impact Publications, 2001)
- *Best Cover Letters For $100,000+ Jobs* (Impact Publications, 2001)

However, this book is not about preparing for your search. Rather, the focus is on how to effectively manage your interviews, be invited back for second interviews, and get the offers. It's all about interviewing to win!

Formula for Success

There are four basic ingredients to getting the position that you want. Each is vital to your success throughout each and every phase of the interview process. Your performance in each of these will be directly compared to those of other applicants applying for the same position and will be closely scrutinized as they pertain to the specific job at hand.

Therefore, in order to leave each interview knowing that you've positioned yourself as one of the strongest candidates, you must demonstrate your proficiency in all four of these areas:

1. **Written qualifications** – the content and appearance of your resume, cover letter, application, and other written communications.
2. **Attitude and behavior** in all your contacts with the organization.
3. **References** and what they say about your performance, qualifications, achievements, personality, behavior, and interpersonal skills.
4. **Personal performance** in the interview.

With the first two, you have almost total control. The time and effort you invest in developing your resume and cover letter are directly proportionate to the number and quality of interviews you are offered. Your attitude and behavior are equally important. Companies want to hire winners who are confident of their ability to perform and deliver positive results. They want to hire individuals who are excited about their organization, energetic, full of new ideas and strategies, and able to quickly build camaraderie with the other members of the executive team and with their staffs. They want to hire successful people. If you can communicate a positive attitude, you have won half the battle.

What your references have to say about you is only partially under your control. Of course, you will have given considerable thought to your selection of references and be quite confident that each will communicate positive messages about your performance, qualifications, capabilities, and value to a prospective employer. However, because you are not present during the actual exchange between prospective employer and reference, you will never know the full extent of each conversation.

Where references can become more difficult to manage is when a prospective employer contacts your current or most recent employer and you have left that position under less than favorable circumstances. In this situation, it can be difficult to anticipate what an individual will say about you. If you are concerned that their comments may be negative, it is highly recommended that you address that issue in the interview, before your prospective employer ever calls that reference. If you bring up the topic, tell your interviewer that you left your most recent position because it had not been a positive experience, then you have a much greater chance of overcoming this potential obstacle than if you simply ignored and left the interviewer to discover it on his own. This certainly does not mean that you should lie or misrepresent what happened. Rather, you want to position the information in the most favorable light possible and, by being up front with the interviewer, the potentially negative impact will be significantly minimized. For more information on dealing with difficult situations, refer to the section on "Overcoming Obstacles to Opportunity" in Chapter 4.

Fact #1

If you do NOT perform well in an interview, no matter your qualifications, chances are likely that you will not be offered the position.

Fact #2

If you are NOT the most qualified candidate for a particular position, but ARE the best interviewee, chances are likely that you'll get the offer.

Your Personal Interview Agenda

The strength of your interviewing skills and your ability to communicate a positive message of success, achievement, and performance are perhaps the most vital to your success and a key factor in outperforming others vying for the same position. In order to give yourself that competitive advantage, you must first understand what your personal agenda must be in each and every interview:

1. To market yourself.
2. To demonstrate your honesty and integrity.

3. To get the job offer (or, at least, an invitation for another round of interviews).

Marketing

As has been, and will be, repeated in this book over and over, job search is marketing. You have a product to sell – yourself. Your challenge is to effectively market, merchandise, advertise, and promote that product to the right audience. And, one of the most critical components of your marketing campaign is your ability to favorably present that product in an interview situation. How can you best highlight the features and benefits of the product? What are the successes and achievements of the product? What is the value of the product to me and my company? Why do I want to buy this product?

The interview platform is yours to answer the questions above and many others. To succeed, you must know that your product is the best and not be afraid to promote it. Job search and interviewing are tremendously competitive today. Those who win not only have the qualifications, but also the confidence in themselves to sell what it is that they have accomplished and the value and expertise they bring to a new company.

Honesty and Integrity

Equally important to your interview success is your ability to demonstrate your honesty and integrity. Be truthful in responding to all interview questions and never provide your interviewer with the opportunity to question your ethics. Demonstrate, through your answers, that you have faced difficult ethical questions and issues in the past, and that you have always maintained your personal level of integrity. No one wants to hire an individual whose honesty and behavior are questionable.

The Offer

The third and perhaps most critical item on your agenda is quite simple – a job offer. Unless this is an informational interview or networking interview, and not a job interview, your primary objective is an offer. And not just a job offer, but a well-compensated offer. This agenda item should be the catalyst throughout your entire job search process and during each interview. There is really no reason to accept an invitation for an interview unless you are seriously seeking an offer.

Remember, however, that offers for executive employment are almost never made during interview #1. Offers will be forthcoming further in the process, after you have learned more about the company and the position, and the company has had the opportunity to learn more about you, your skills, qualifications, achievements, and value to their organization.

Interview Preparation

To prepare for an interview, you must:

- Remember that interviewing is selling. You are there to promote a product – yourself – highlight its features and benefits, and position yourself for a new career opportunity.

- Research everything that you can about the company you will be interviewing with and the position you will be interviewing for. The Internet has now made this a remarkably easy task.

- Appear confident and enthusiastic with a high level of energy and impeccable ethics.

- Dress the part of the executive, act the part, and display the appropriate behaviors.

- Remember that interviewing is a two-way street. Not only is the company interviewing you, you are interviewing them. Will you be proud to work for this company? Do you like the environment? Do you like the people? What are the long-term opportunities?

- Remember that the interviewer's primary goal during interview #1 is to identify prime candidates and eliminate unqualified ones.

- Remember that your primary objective in interview #1 is an invitation to interview #2. Your secondary objective in interview #1 and all subsequent interviews is, of course, a job offer.

Be Prepared!

Materials You Will Need

Arrive at each interview with either a leather portfolio or briefcase that contains:

- additional copies of your resume, career portfolio, and any other printed materials you may want to share
- your laptop if you plan to share electronic or online information (and if it is appropriate in the particular interview situation)
- letters of recommendation and referral
- copies of outstanding performance reviews
- copies of a select number of honors and awards
- press clippings (features and articles you authored or were featured in)
- a plain pad of paper for note-taking
- at least three pens
- your current business cards (if applicable)

It's Okay to Take Notes!

Not only is it okay to take notes, it is strongly recommended. When you take a moment to jot down a few thoughts, you are demonstrating your interest in the company and the position. You are showing your interviewer that you are really listening to what she is saying.

Furthermore, these notes will be the foundation for your subsequent "thank-you-for-the-interview" letter which is discussed in detail in Chapter 7. At this point, let it suffice to say that your thank-you letters should be written as powerful marketing tools, a continuation of your resume, cover letter, and interview. Of course you want to express your appreciation for the interview, but, more importantly, you want to clearly reiterate the qualifications, achievements, and track record of success that you bring to the position based on the company's specific needs. For example, if during the interview there was a great deal of discussion regarding the instability of the workforce, you would then focus much of your thank-you letter on how you've dealt with instability and change in the past, the actions you initiated, and their positive results. Note-taking during the interview will help you remember issues that were addressed, problems the company is facing, and challenges to be met, so you can address the most pressing items in your letter.

The greatest benefit of thank-you letters is their ability to distinguish you from other candidates who send a more traditional and less action-oriented thank-you letter. With your letter, you've demonstrated a sincere interest in the organization and already demonstrated your ability to respond to their needs. They will be impressed and intrigued!

Overview of the Interview Process

The interview process is generally initiated through your efforts in contacting a company or a recruiter. Either you are aware of a specific opportunity, have been recommended by one of your network contacts or simply contacted the organization to express your interest in executive employment opportunities. Your contact will sometimes begin with a telephone call; other times, by forwarding your resume and cover letter.

Once the company or recruiter has received your materials, they will be closely reviewed. Do you have the qualifications for the position they advertised or for an anticipated future opportunity? Are you the type of individual they would be interested in interviewing and perhaps hiring? Do you present a unique set of skills and qualifications? Do you have contacts that may be of value to the organization? Is the company anticipating growth and expansion, dictating the need for additional executive talent? Is one of their current executives planning to retire or leave the company shortly?

If the company's answer to any of the above questions is yes, and they are impressed by your written qualifications, chances are the next step will be a preliminary interview in the form of a telephone screening. This is particularly true for candidates who live out-of-state. Prior to the company investing money to bring you in for a personal interview, an initial telephone screening will generally be conducted to determine if (1) you have the right qualifications and (2) you have the right attitude and personality.

If you pass the initial telephone screening, a date and time for a personal interview will be scheduled. Refer to the sections titled "Types of Interviews" and "Interview Situations" in Chapter 3 to learn about the various interview scenarios that may present themselves. You can think of the telephone screening (Interview #1) as a preliminary test to determine if you possess the skills, qualifications, and experiences that the company is seeking in a qualified candidate. You can assume that if you pass this phase of the interview process, you will be invited for a face-to-face interview (Interview #2).

> Your Objective in Interview #1 **(Telephone-Screening Interview)** is Straightforward:
>
> An Invitation for Interview #2 **(In-Person Interview)**

How many interviews can you expect before an offer is put on the table? That is a very difficult question to answer. There may be instances where, after only two interviews, you are presented with an offer. However, considering the level of position you are seeking as a senior executive, it is more likely that there will be multiple interviews long before an offer is ever made.

Virtually every senior management and executive job seeker can expect to interview with other senior executives of the hiring company. This would include the CEO, president, CFO, human resources director and perhaps executive vice presidents of specific operating functions (e.g., sales, marketing, manufacturing, customer service, product development, administration, information technology). You may also be asked to interview with members of or the entire board of directors, the company's bankers or their investor group, their strategic business partners, and others with a vested interest. Obviously, the more senior the position, the more intense and widespread the interview process becomes.

When an offer is finally presented, you can be assured that all interested parties (or, at least, most) have communicated their interest in you. You should feel confident that you will have their support once you begin your new position and that the majority of individuals believed you to be the most qualified for the assignment. Thus, you can begin your new job with confidence, certainty, and anticipation of great things to come.

Practice, Practice, and Then Practice

How many individuals can walk into an interview situation poised, relaxed, and confident in their ability? For individuals who are naturally charming, interesting, and comfortable in what can be somewhat threatening situations, interviews are generally no problem. These individuals tend to have strong communication and interpersonal skills, and naturally exude confidence and success.

Most people, however, are not natural charmers and, more often than not, are somewhat intimidated in an interview situation. This is particularly true if they have been in the job market for an extended period of time, are beginning to feel the financial impact, and starting to question their own value and self-worth. It is a natural inclination to be anxious before the interview (you really need this job!) and begin to question your own qualifications (why has no one hired me yet?).

Performing well in an interview does not mean changing who you are. Rather, it means that you must clearly identify your obstacles to interview success and work to minimize them in each interview situation. The first step in this process is to be honest with yourself. Are you confident in an interview? Can you answer the difficult questions? Can you overcome objections? Can you competitively position yourself against other candidates? Can you play to win?

To overcome these obstacles and become a more polished and confident interviewer, practice is essential. Just as with any other task, you can positively influence and enhance your performance and results through preparation and rehearsal. Practice will help you to become much better organized and clearer in your thought process, providing you with the knowledge to answer the expected questions correctly and with confidence.

Being a bit nervous in an interview situation is expected. In fact, the adrenaline gives you the energy and the edge to perform. Ask any stage actor or theatrical performer. They will tell you that they continue to experience stage fright even after years of live performances, but have learned to harness that anxiety into positive energy. Interview situations are much the same. Realize that the nervousness sharpens your senses and can be the catalyst for some of your best performances ever.

For practice interviews you can ask a friend, relative, or colleague for assistance. You want to simulate an interview situation as closely as possible by creating a physical environment much like that of an interview – a private area or room with desk or table and two chairs. Forget that you know each other and begin the practice session with a welcoming handshake and a few brief moments of light conversation, much as you will experience in an actual interview. Then use the interview questions in Chapter 5 as your practice guide to actually conduct mock interviews and practice your answers.

You might also consider approaching another professional who is currently in an active job search campaign to be your interview practice partner. This is a great way for both of you to have the opportunity to practice, brainstorm, and refine each other's interview performance.

Finally, if you believe that your interviewing skills require major surgery, consider hiring a career counselor or coach. These individuals are well trained in interviewing and can provide you with substantive feedback and direction to enhance your performance. For an investment of potentially only a few hundred dollars, a counselor or coach can often help you make a dramatically positive difference in your interview success and, in turn, the number of offers you will receive.

Whomever you select as your interview partner, it is imperative that you devote the time and energy that is necessary to fine-tune your interviewing skills and your answers. Go over questions time and time again until you feel confident in your responses, the messages you convey, and the manner in which you communicate. Rehearsals are great. You can stop and start as many times as you like until your answers are second nature. With real interviews you do not have that luxury, so make sure that you are 100% prepared each and every time.

First Impressions Still Count!

All of our lives we've been taught that first impressions count and leave a lasting impression. At no time is this more apparent than in the job search and interview process. In these situations, first impressions are vital and are based on four specific observations:

1. **Punctuality.** If you're late, you're usually out of the running. There are virtually no excuses for late arrivals (barring unforeseen emergencies). Give yourself plenty of time and then some. In fact, arriving a few minutes early allows you the opportunity to collect your thoughts, take a deep breath, relax, and get ready.

2. **Appropriate business attire.** Modern yet conservative clothing is the recommendation – nothing too flashy or faddish. When your interviewer takes his first glance, you want him to note that you are sharp, classy, and a cut above the competition. Even if companies boast of casual working environments, the interview is not the time for casual!

3. **Personal grooming habits.** Scraggly beards, unkempt hair, and facial piercings are out of the question! Need I say more?

4. **Self-confidence.** A warm smile, direct eye contact, and a firm handshake make a positive and lasting impression.

If you make a good first impression, your interview will get off to a positive start. However, if your first impression "is less than desirable, most likely you have lost the opportunity within just seconds of your arrival. Whether right or wrong, people's perceptions drive their decision making. Don't let a poor initial impression ruin your chances of what could be a great opportunity.

Top 9 Strategies for Interview Success

Following are the top nine strategic and tactical tips to enhance your interviewing skills. If you can master them, you will outperform your competition and position yourself for an outstanding executive opportunity. Read these strategies carefully and be sure to integrate them, as appropriate, into the responses you give to each and every interview question.

1. **Sell it to me ... don't tell it to me.** Interviewing is basically a selling game. You have a product to promote – yourself – and your goal is to market that product as effectively as possible. Don't just TELL your interviewer that "Yes, I managed annual budgeting for the division." Rather, SELL the fact that "For the past six years I have managed the entire budgeting function for a $22 million operating division, initiated a series of cost-reduction programs, and cut $2.5 million from the bottom line." You've sold the success, not just told the facts!

2. **Transition each negative to a positive.** Suppose someone inquires as to your proficiency with Excel. You know that you have never touched the program. However, you certainly do not want to blurt out, "No, I'm not familiar with it." Rather, transition the negative to a positive with the following. "I have used spread-

sheet applications throughout my career and am most familiar with Lotus. I'm sure getting a good handle on Excel won't take long at all."

3. **Use the "big-to-little strategy."** Putting some structure into your interview responses will make the process much easier and more manageable for you. Begin your answers with a big response and then use specific little examples to demonstrate your proficiency. Consider the following example. Your interviewer inquires about your experience in managing information technology resources. Your response begins with the big: "Throughout the past 12 years, I have held full strategic planning, operating, and management responsibility for a 48-person information resources organization." Then, proceed with the particulars, the little: "Specific highlights that may interest you include a $3.8 million investment in IT hardware, introduction of both Internet and intranet technologies, and the successful start-up of a global telecommunications network."

4. **Use function to demonstrate scope of responsibility and achievement.** If your interviewer inquires about your daily functional responsibility as Senior Director of Human Resources, do not just provide a laundry list of tasks. Rather, use this opportunity to communicate the scope of your responsibility. For example, "As HR Director, I managed the entire HR function for a 2,200-employee corporation. I introduced new compensation plans throughout six manufacturing locations, created a unique incentive program for all levels of management, negotiated favorable union contracts governing over 90% of our workforce, and facilitated the acquisition and introduction of PeopleSoft to enhance our IT capabilities."

5. **Be confident in the fact that you've already passed the first test.** If you are interviewing either in a face-to-face situation or over the telephone, be confident that you have already passed the preliminary review of your skills, qualifications, and experience. If you

hadn't, you would not be interviewing! Therefore, approach the interview with enthusiasm and security in the fact that you have the basic qualifications. Now your challenge is to sell, negotiate, close, and win!

6. **Remain in the realm of reality.** Everyone pushes the envelope a bit when interviewing. You're there to promote yourself, sell your success, highlight your achievements, and get a job offer. However, always live by the motto, *"Remain in the realm of reality."* Every single thing you communicate on your resume or in an interview must be 100% accurate, truthful, and verifiable. Only push so far. If you go beyond reality, you will have lost the opportunity.

7. **Take the initiative.** If there is information that you believe is important to communicate to your interviewer, be sure to take the initiative and introduce the topic into the conversation when appropriate. If you are nearing the end of your interview and the topic has never been addressed, tell your interviewer that there are several other points you would like to address and ask if now is the appropriate time. The onus is on you to take the initiative.

8. **Be positive, confident, and self-assured.** Companies want to hire winners, and winners communicate an immediate message of confidence in their abilities. Be sure that you convey this message through both your verbal and nonverbal communications. A strong handshake, direct eye contact, and a smile readily communicate self-assurance and poise.

9. **Listen carefully.** In any interview situation, you are there to answer questions, provide information, explore the opportunity, highlight your success, and market your qualifications. However, just as important, you are there to listen to your interviewer, understand his concerns, and directly respond to those issues.

This can be a difficult challenge because so much of your energy is focused on answering the interviewer's questions as opposed to hearing what the interviewer is saying.

Your interviewer will most likely communicate a great deal of information about the position, the company, the major issues impacting the company, the need to fill the position, and the qualifications for the ideal candidate. Listen carefully to all of this information. Then use it wisely in positioning your responses, and later, in writing your thank-you letter. If your interviewer knows that you are really listening to what he is saying, you will immediately demonstrate a message of your interest and commitment. People want to hire other people who understand them, support them, and are sensitive to their needs. Position yourself above the crowd by not only communicating your competencies, but responding to the organization's and your interviewer's specific needs.

3

Types of Interviews

N OW THAT YOU HAVE devoted the necessary time
and energy to preparing for your interviews, practic-
ing your answers and refining your presentation style,
you are ready to move forward. Most important, you
must understand the various types and styles of interview situations you may encounter, which can best be summarized as follows:

Interview Styles:
- Traditional
- Behavioral
- Situational

Interview Types:
- Informational/Networking Interviews
- Screening Interviews
- Hiring Interview (the most important!)

Each type and style has a unique purpose and strategy; each affords you the opportunity to market yourself, sell your achievements, and position yourself for a challenging new executive opportunity. The remainder of this chapter will discuss each interview style and type in detail, giving you the information and "insider tips" you will need in order to transition yourself from an "average" interviewee into an extraordinarily well-prepared candidate who is able to perform with confidence in any type of interview situation.

Traditional Interviews

Traditional interviews are what you will most likely expect to encounter and, quite often, what you will encounter. These types of interviews are what normally come to mind when you think about interviewing – a situation where a prospective employer will be asking you specific questions about yourself, your work experience, skills, qualifications, achievements, project highlights, industry experience, technical competencies, educational credentials, technical certifications, and more. Your interviewer will ask questions and you will respond with factual information about what you have done, what you can do, and the value that you bring to their organization.

Situational and Behavioral Interviews

Situational and behavioral interviews have taken the traditional interview and expanded it into new directions in an effort to strengthen and improve the interviewing process. The rationale for these types of interviews is that past performance is the best indicator of future performance, success, and achievement. Therefore, if an interviewer is able to ask questions that require job seekers to articulate how they would perform and how they did perform in past situations, it will provide them with more accurate information upon which to make smart and effective hiring decisions.

To differentiate between the two concepts of situational and behavioral interviews, both of which are based on your behavior in certain circumstances, consider the following:

> **Situational** interviews focus on what a job seeker would do in a specific situation.
>
> **Behavioral** interviews focus on what a job seeker did do in a specific situation.

Today, both have become a staple of the hiring process and every job seeker should be prepared to encounter and effectively respond to these types of questions on a routine basis. In fact, situational and behavioral interviewing is becoming the norm for most companies and most positions. Who can argue with the fact that past performance really is the best indicator of future performance? Therefore, if you want to hire someone who can perform to your expectations, why not focus on how that person has performed in similar situations in the past? It only seems logical.

In preparing yourself for these types of interviews, begin by thinking carefully about your past experience, performance milestones, special projects, and more. Then, select 10-15 different stories, examples, or achievements that demonstrate your specific qualifications for the position at hand and be prepared to share them during the interview either as a behavioral response (*"This is what I did do in that particular situation"*) or as a situational response (*"I would do such-and-such in a situation like that, just as I did when I encountered _____"*).

Three great strategies to help you develop your stories are the CAR, OAR, and STAR methods:

CAR – **Challenge, Action, Result** – What challenge did you meet, what specific action did you initiate to meet it, and what was the positive result?

OAR – **Opportunity, Action, Result** – What specific opportunity did you identify and develop, what specific action did you take to do that, and what was the positive result?

STAR – **Situation, Task, Action, Result** – What was the specific situation you encountered, what action did you take, and what was the positive result?

When you put "structure" into your stories (as with the CAR, OAR, and STAR methods), you will be able to more easily remember and communicate them in a concise and easy-to-understand manner to your interviewer. What's more, you'll be focusing your entire interview on what you have accomplished in the past (behavioral) and what value you'll deliver to the company in the future (situational).

Note that many experts consider situational and behavioral interviewing to be one and the same, while others look at the two as different styles. It should be readily apparent from our discussion that the two are closely interwoven, and whether you consider them the same or different styles, both are based on how you behave and what you do (or would do). Most important, you must realize these types of interviews are more often the norm these days and you must be prepared.

In summarizing our discussion of situational and behavioral interviews, it is important to appreciate the fact that they really aren't anything new. What's new is that these styles have been further expanded, formally recognized, and named. Think about a job interview you might have had 10 years ago which you, most likely, considered a "traditional" interview. Weren't you asked questions about what you would do in a particular situation? Most likely, your answer is yes. And weren't you asked to discuss or demonstrate specific behaviors that you had previously displayed in the workplace? Again, your answer is probably yes. So, back to my original point that situational and behavioral interviewing aren't really new; they're simply refined, expanded, and now considered an alternative and enhanced method of interviewing.

One final note before we move on to the various types of interviews. Whether you are engaged in a traditional, behavioral, and situational interview session, remember the following: Interviewing really has never changed! It's still all about building rapport, understanding and responding to the company's and interviewer's needs, clearly communicating your qualifications, and positioning yourself as the #1 candidate.

Informational/Networking Interviews

These types of interviews are often overlooked, but can be a valuable tool in the initial planning and development stages of your executive job search program. Informational and networking interviews provide you with the opportunity to explore new career paths, professions, industries, and markets by meeting with/speaking with individuals directly involved in those disciplines. Most significant, you want to uncover the specific skills, qualifications, and competencies that such companies require of their executive candidates. It is a time of exploration, research, and information collection to provide you with the background critical to identifying "how" you want to position yourself, "where" you want to position yourself, and "who" you want to be. These interviews can also be a springboard for direct referrals to specific opportunities.

> Whether you are engaged in a traditional, behavioral, and situational interview session, always remember the following: Interviewing really has never changed! It's still all about building rapport, understanding and responding to the company's and interviewer's needs, clearly communicating your qualifications, and positioning yourself as the #1 candidate.

Similar to when you are building your personal network of contacts, approach these types of interviews with a query for help and assistance – NOT a specific job. And, just as with your other networking efforts, allow your market reach to be broad. Contact friends, relatives, acquaintances, colleagues, co-workers, managers and even strangers to identify opportunities for networking or informational interviews. Although these individuals may not have a direct lead or opportunity, each has his/her own personal network of contacts that you can leverage to further expand and accelerate your campaign.

Never think that informational and networking interviews are a waste of time. In addition to providing you with information regarding new industries, positions, and career opportunities, these types of interviews can result in formal job interviews (if an opportunity exists), a referral to someone else within that individual's company, or a referral to an outside contact.

Screening Interviews – Phone or Electronic

Screening interviews are just what they imply. A particular job opportunity exists and step #1 in the company's interview process is to screen potential candidates into or out of consideration. These types of interviews have become a norm in today's competitive market where it is not unusual for a company to receive 200, 500, 700, or even 1,000 resumes in response to a specific opportunity, many of which are from applicants nationwide. The interviewer's goal is to review resumes, select candidates who meet the company's basic hiring requirements for that specific opportunity, and then conduct preliminary interviews to ascertain if, indeed, an individual has the right qualifications and is the type of candidate the company is seeking. Screening interviews are a quick, efficient, and low-cost strategy for companies to narrow down their list of applicants to just a select few to be brought in for face-to-face interviews. They are usually short in duration, dictated by a specific set of questions, and have one objective in mind – exclusion of inappropriate candidates.

Screening interviews can be conducted via telephone, in person or through the use of electronic technology. The higher the level of position you are seeking, the more likely that you will be screened either by phone or in person. These types of interviews not only give your interviewer specific information regarding your skills, performance, employment history, and competencies, but also allow the interviewer to get a sense of who you are, how you communicate, how you interact, and if you might "fit" into their corporate culture. Technology-based screenings (via a PC, the Internet or email) are generally for younger, less experienced personnel where screening is based largely on specific skills and measurable qualifications. These types of screening interviews are totally unbiased, asking the exact same questions in the same tone of voice and in the same order to each and every potential hire. Further, the computer can instantaneously score your answers and determine whether or not you should be asked to proceed with the interview process.

Bear in mind that these types of screening interviews are not the norm for senior executives, although as technology continues to expand, it is inevitable that they will become a more widely used executive screening tool.

If a prospective employer phones you to obtain additional information, you can assume that this is a screening interview. Treat it seriously, as you would any other interview. What information you communicate to this individual (despite the limited amount of time), how it is presented, your tone, your attitude, and your energy are all important considerations as to whether or not you will be invited for a personal interview.

Most of these calls will come unexpectedly. To ensure that you are ALWAYS prepared, keep a working space available right by your telephone. Not only will you need paper and pen, it is advisable that you keep an index card file readily accessible. This file should contain the names and addresses of all of your job contacts, information about available positions, dates you forwarded your resume and cover letter, and other specific information. Also keep a copy of your resume available for quick and easy reference. Do not allow a prospective employer to ever catch you unprepared. If you do, chances are you will lose the opportunity.

If you are invited for a face-to-face screening interview, you will most likely be meeting with one of the company's human resource professionals or with an outside recruiter. The agenda is the same as if completed on the telephone – to get basic information and determine whether or not you have the qualifications required for the position. A face-to-face interview is a much more valuable preliminary tool, allowing the interviewer to not only hear your responses, but see "who you are." In addition, these types of screenings are a much better opportunity for you to sell yourself. Generally, face-to-face screening interviews are offered only to candidates within the local geographic region. Rarely is a company going to absorb the expense of bringing a candidate in from out of town if they have not first conducted a preliminary telephone screening.

You may also experience face-to-face screening interviews at job fairs. These types of interviews are usually quite brief as a result of the large number of potential applicants. In addition, many recruiters will conduct screenings to (1) determine if you are an appropriate candidate for a current search assignment, (2) determine if you might be a candidate for one of their client companies, although no active search is underway, (3) obtain additional information for future opportunities, or (4) get other candidate referrals from you.

Hiring Interviews

Hiring interviews are what most executive job search candidates consider the norm in interviewing. They are comprehensive interviews (generally after you have passed the screening interview) designed to allow you and the interviewer to explore your qualifications in much greater depth. These interviews are the first step in positioning yourself for a new career opportunity.

It is critical to remember that hiring interviews are two-way streets. Not only are you there to answer the interviewer's questions and sell your qualifications, you are also there with your own personal agenda. Is this the type of organization you want to work for? Does the company appear to be financially stable? What is the company's current market position? What are their key issues? What are their goals? Do you believe that you could deliver value to this organization? Would you be proud to work for them? Is it the "right" environment for you?

If your answers to these questions are negative, even though your interaction with the interviewer was positive, you may not want to take the opportunity any further. No need to waste your time or theirs. The only value in sustaining the relationship at this point is that (1) you believe that your issues can be addressed and resolved or (2) you believe that by continuing the interview process you may be able to obtain referrals and leads for other opportunities.

Hiring interviews generally take place in an office setting, but can be structured in one of five basic formats:

- one-on-one interviews
- serial interviews
- sequential interviews
- panel interviews
- candidate group interviews
- out-of-the-office interviews

One-On-One Interviews

One-on-one, face-to-face interviews are the most common. While screening interviews are generally conducted by a human resource professional, hiring interviews are generally conducted by a decision maker – someone on either the senior or executive management team. Understand at this point that you will be asked very specific questions about your past employment experiences, responsibilities, accountabilities, projects, achievements, skills, and qualifications. Although largely focusing on your professional experience, hiring interviews will also attempt to obtain relevant personal information about your management or leadership style, commitment, drive, energy, interests, and personal character.

Serial Interviews

Serial interviews are similar to one-on-one interviews. The only difference is that you are scheduled, in advance, to meet with a number of individuals, one right after the other. No decision is made as to your qualifications until such time that all interviews have been completed and the interviewers compare their notes and observations, making their recommendations whether to eliminate you from consideration, invite you to continue in the interview process, or make you an offer of employment.

These types of interviews can be exhausting. It is not unusual to start your day at 9 a.m. and not finish until 4 or 5 p.m. Your greatest challenge is to maintain your energy and drive throughout every session. Approach each interview as your first, highlighting your core qualifications and achievements, and communicating your value to the organization. Remember that each interviewer will have his/her own agenda, so be sure to be responsive to the specific questions and issues at hand.

Sequential Interviews

Sequential interviews are now the norm for senior executive positions. They also are one-on-one interviews conducted over a period of time – days, weeks, or even months. If, after completing hiring interview #1, you are still under consideration, you will be invited back for interview #2, then #3, etc., until everyone in the organization who wants or needs to interview you has done so, the company has determined that you are THE candidate and they make you an employment offer.

Sequential interviews are progressive, allowing you the opportunity to move forward in the hiring process, ask more intelligent questions as you delve further into the company and its operations, and provide each interviewer with more detail to substantiate your qualifications.

Sequential interviews tend to be with different people, again with their own agendas, questions, issues, and concerns. Your challenge is to provide information, ask questions, and sell the interviewer on your qualifications, value, and candidacy. This is much easier to accomplish in sequential interviews as opposed to serial interviews. You are able to keep your enthusiasm high and your responses fresh because you have the time to prepare and energize between each interview.

Panel Interviews

These types of interviews can be the most intimidating. You can often feel as though it is you "against" all of them. Not only is the concept frightening, the physical environment and layout of the room can be threatening. You often feel pressured and under a great deal of stress. You've got one opportunity – and generally only one – to impress the entire group of panelists. Further, in this type of interview situation, it is often difficult for you to have much control. Although you may respond to one panelist's question and believe that he/she thought your answer to be quite appropriate, you are not aware of how the other panelists have interpreted your responses. Each person is there with his/her own agenda, making it difficult for you to respond to each individual person's concerns while meeting the concerns of all the other panelists.

The best strategy to succeed in this type of interview situation is to relax, be yourself, be confident in your abilities, and work to clearly communicate your value. Realize that the chances are unlikely that you will meet every panelist's requirements 100%. It's okay. This is a group decision-making process, generally not dependent upon the opinions or recommendations of just one individual. Be sure to make eye contact with each and every panelist throughout the interview session, demonstrating your interest, your response to their specific needs, and your ability to function in a high-pressure, stressful environment.

Candidate Group Interviews

It is unlikely that in your search for an executive position you will ever be faced with a group interview situation – when a company interviews a number of candidates in one large group setting. These types of interviews are generally conducted for less experienced personnel when a company is attempting to evaluate the qualifications, interpersonal relations, and communication skills of each candidate. How do they interact with their peers? What is their communication style? Are they easily intimidated? Do they take control? Are they polished in their presentation? By utilizing group interviewing strategies, companies are attempting to identify candidates that not only meet the qualifications of the position, but are confident and positive with a winning attitude.

Out-Of-The-Office Interviews

Taking a prospective employee out to lunch or dinner is a great way to get to know them. The situation is more casual and the candidate is more relaxed. There is less structure and less stress. Companies will often use this tactic to get a glimpse into the "real" person – how they interact and communicate with others. These types of interviews are generally in the latter stages of the interview process, after you have already demonstrated that you have the basic qualifications for the position and after the company has already begun to consider you a top candidate. However, with the hectic pace so many of us keep today, mealtime interviews are increasing in frequency simply because of ease and efficient time management. No matter how casual the situation or the environment, always remember that out-of-the-office interviews are just that – interviews. Every word, gesture, and mannerism will be closely observed and scrutinized.

Types of Interview Questions

There are two basic types of interview questions:

Direct Questions are:

- The most common type of interview questions.
- Specific questions requiring specific answers.
- Asked in a planned sequence and structure.
- Either closed or open-ended.
- Designed to explore specifics regarding your work experience, educational credentials, career objectives, special skills, technical proficiencies, strengths and weaknesses.

Examples:

"Are you PC literate?"

"What was your greatest achievement at IBM?"

"Are you willing to travel as the job may require?"

"How do you manage disgruntled, unmotivated staff?"

"How much was the largest budget you managed?"

"What was the largest number of staff you ever had reporting to you?"

Indirect Questions are:

- Less common than direct questions.
- Less structured than direct questions.
- Generally open-ended, providing you with the opportunity to elaborate on your skills, experiences, projects, achievements, and career successes.

Examples:

"Tell me about yourself."

"Have you ever been involved in merger activities?"

"What are your long-term career goals?"

"Can you define your leadership style?"

"Are you an effective problem solver?"

"What motivates you?"

An effective executive job seeker is prepared for any type of interview, any type of question, and any type of environment. Be sure that you thoroughly understand your product (YOU) and how to best present that product across a variety of situations.

4

Overcoming Obstacles to Opportunity

I nterviewing can present a vast range of challenges no matter the position, the company, or your background. One of the greatest challenges of all is learning to favorably present unfavorable situations. For example, how can you explain why you were fired from your last position without closing the door on your next opportunity? How can you explain why you are currently in a position several grades lower than that which you previously held? How will you counter the fact that the recommendation from your past supervisor is anything but flattering? What do you tell someone when they ask why you haven't worked for over a year?

These questions, and others like them, present you with unique interviewing challenges. You know that your primary goal is to market your qualifications, performance, and success in order to land your next position. Bottom line, you're in the interview to sell yourself. However, situations like the ones above tend to make an interview much more complex since chances are that your interviewer will want to focus a great deal of the interview on your particular situation. So, what can you do to overcome these difficult issues, refocus the interview on your core skills and competencies, and still keep yourself in the running, particularly when the competition is so fierce?

Interview Challenge #1
You've Been Fired

Let us suppose that you were fired from your last position as Executive Vice President of Production for a $300 million plastics manufacturer. You had been recruited two years earlier to plan and orchestrate the turnaround of the business. The company was suffering from significant financial, customer, and market share losses, and was on the edge of bankruptcy. Your challenge was to restructure operations, introduce new products, expand market penetration, retrain staff, and redesign core business processes. Further, there were major issues between the other executives – all family members. After two years, and with no notice, you were fired on a Monday morning. How can you present this in a positive light? Here's how:

> *"When I joined the company, I was challenged to lead the organization through a massive operating turnaround and market repositioning to restore profitability. The company had lost more than $70 million over the past two years in addition to many of its major customers. Morale was low, product quality was poor, and there was uncer-*

tainty as to whether the company could survive. Through my efforts and those of my staff, we were able to effectuate a positive turnaround, halt losses, and deliver the first profits in over three years. We redesigned major product lines, revitalized our image in the market, restored credibility within the financial community, and positioned the company to return to its position as a major competitor.

Unfortunately, I was not able to resolve the in-fighting among the family members and their constant battle over money and control. As such, I often found myself in a position of mediating between family members and being forced to take sides on one issue after another. It was an extremely difficult situation. No matter my course of action and regardless of our strong financial results, there was always a family member who felt as though I had betrayed him. I could never win. Then one morning, with no notice, two of the family members called me in, handed me my severance agreement, and escorted me out the door. These two individuals had wanted to expand our sales into Europe. I, and several others, had determined that it was premature at this point and made the decision to keep our sales domestic for at least one more year. Obviously, this decision did not sit well with those two family members who, coincidentally, owned 60% of the company. I was immediately let go."

Interview Success Strategy:
Transition a negative into a positive.

The candidate was honest (he was fired), but presented it in the most positive way possible with the emphasis on the success of the turnaround and revitalization of the company.

Interview Challenge #2 –
You're Overqualified for Your Current Job

Consider the following scenario. After five years as CFO of an emerging biomedical technology company, the investors pulled out, the technology was acquired, and the company was closed. With two kids in college and another a junior in high school, you needed a job immediately. Your savings had dwindled over the years and your wife's nursing job simply could not support the family. You were nervous and jumped at the first opportunity – a Controller position with a $150 million automotive products distributor. The position was 20 minutes from your home, and although you took a cut in pay, the ease and immediacy were well worth it. Now a year has passed and you are secure in your position, but you're bored and unchallenged. It's time for a change and time to get back to a top-level financial position. How do you explain all of this favorably without communicating the fact that you felt desperate at that time? Here's how:

"I accepted the Controller position for one reason and one reason only – it was a unique opportunity to demonstrate the transferability of my skills from one industry to another. My entire career thus far had been in the biomedical, computer, and telecommunications technology industries, and I was curious. How did other, non-technical industries operate? Were their financial needs so vastly different? Were their cost structures and budgeting processes unique? How much influence did industry specialization have on the broader functions of strategic planning, change management, and performance improvement? I wanted the chance to try my hand at something different from what I had been exposed to in the past.

"Well the last year has been quite a challenge. I have learned that, although the financial, accounting, budgeting, asset management and risk management processes are quite different, the underlying financial management strategies are quite similar. In turn, I have not only met my objectives, but exceeded them, introducing several novel financial and technical systems to more effectively manage our operations. Most notably, I decentralized budgeting, reduced operating costs $12 million annually, introduced sophisticated client/server technologies, and reallocated over $50 million in assets to support new product development.

"Now, however, I am ready for new challenges where I can again assume the level of financial and leadership responsibility which I have held in the past. I will look back upon my tenure here as a wonderful learning experience."

Interview Success Strategy:
Bring the value of the experience to the forefront and pull attention away from the lessened level of responsibility.

In this situation, the candidate focused on highlighting the unique aspects of the opportunity (e.g., industry diversification, responsibilities, new projects, new challenges) and its value in strengthening his executive skill set. By doing so, the fact that the position was of lesser responsibility became diminished in the interviewer's mind.

Interview Challenge #3 –
Your References are Poor

When you were hired by your current employer in 1999, you knew it was a great opportunity. Coming in as Regional Sales Manager, you earned six promotions in six years and advanced to your most recent position as Vice President of Sales for the North American market. Your career with the company was outstanding, except for your last position. A new EVP for Worldwide Sales was recruited in 2002 and, immediately upon his arrival, made massive organizational and staffing changes. Because of your tenure with the company, you were one of a select group of senior sales executives that was retained.

However, the situation became increasingly difficult as it was obvious that the new EVP was not pleased to have been forced to retain some of the existing management team. Virtually overnight, your sales quotas and profit objectives were doubled. If it had been in the earlier years, you would have had no problem making the numbers. However, the market is quite mature now and growth at that pace is totally unrealistic. As such, for the first time since joining the company, you were not able to make your numbers, and the EVP finally prevailed. On August 14, 2004, you were let go. How do you explain this without it appearing so negative? Here's how:

"In anticipation that you will be speaking with my most recent supervisor, I would like to make a few comments. I'm sure that Mr. Smith will tell you that I did not make my sales or profit objectives in 2003, that my performance was off track, and that my commitment to the company was questionable. He will probably also mention that there was a severe lack of synergy between my style of sales management and his leadership objectives.

"I cannot argue any of these points. However, I can comment that prior to Mr. Smith's arrival with the company, I delivered a minimum of 120% of my quota for six consecutive years. Not only did my team achieve aggressive revenue and profit goals, I built what has now become known as the company's model sales organization. We were aggressive, we were successful, and we were virtually unstoppable. Unfortunately, all of that changed in 2002 when new leadership arrived and sought to replace the entire executive sales management team. Because of my numbers and track record of performance, I was selected as one of only six senior sales executives offered the opportunity to remain with the company. I accepted the new challenge, restaffed my organization, and attempted to move forward. However, the environment was not particularly supportive and there was an earnest desire to bring new talent in.

"I worked tirelessly over the next year to demonstrate my value to the new leadership team and my continued commitment to the organization. However, their goals included a complete restaffing of the entire sales organization. To ensure that would happen, the sales and profit quotas for each remaining executive were doubled while our budgets and resources were slashed. It was a no-win situation for everyone.

"I look back at the experience with no bitterness. An great track record of performance with a prestigious company is an asset to anyone's career. It certainly has been to mine. I hope that you will take all of this information under advisement as you speak with Mr. Smith regarding my performance. I would also request that you contact Mr. Green, a long-time member of the executive team, who will be delighted to share information about my entire career with the company and can be honest about my years of success."

Interview Success Strategy:
Shift the focus to positive performance and results.

The strategy here is to be honest and explain the reason for the negative reference in as positive a light as possible. Be sure to focus on the results you delivered despite the often-difficult working environment. Then, be sure to provide full contact information for someone else (preferably someone else in the same company) who can accurately communicate the quality of your performance.

Interview Challenge #4 –
You Haven't Worked for a Year

This is every job seeker's worst nightmare – unemployment for an extended period of time. Let's suppose you were a veteran of IBM and that you worked for the company for more than 10 years. You advanced rapidly through a series of increasingly responsible manufacturing management positions to your final assignment directing all new manufacturing ventures and partnerships throughout Asia and Latin America. It was great. However, as the organization downsized, rightsized, and reconfigured itself, you were caught in a massive layoff.

Your initial reaction was "No problem." With so many years of experience, you assumed your job search would be easy to manage. You were realistic, understanding that it would take some time, numerous contacts, and an aggressive job search campaign. But you were optimistic.

Now, 13 months later, you're still in the market. How do you explain the situation without appearing undesirable? Here's how:

"When I left IBM, I decided to take a short break after more than 20 years of steady employment. I wanted to spend some time with my family over the summer months, visit friends I had not seen in years, and take a few computer courses to brush up on my hands-on skills. The time was invaluable to re-energize my mind, my heart, and my soul.

"I then spent several months planning my job search, evaluating my career options, and exploring the possibility of employment within upstate New York. At that time, I was not particularly interested in relocating my family. Rochester had been our home throughout my career. Unfortunately, as I'm sure you are aware, the Rochester market has been extremely hard hit as a result of the layoffs at IBM, Eastman Kodak, and several other large corporations. Employment opportunities are virtually non-existent at the level of position which I am seeking.

"Several months into my research and preparation it became obvious that I would have to consider relocation. Never one to forge ahead blindly, I spent a good deal of time investigating other geographic areas in the U.S. to determine which markets were strongest, which markets offered the best public education opportunities, and which areas would be of interest both personally and professionally.

"I then began to conduct a serious job search, about seven to eight months after leaving IBM. As such, I have been actively seeking a new executive opportunity for about five months now and have been fortunate to have been offered about 10-12 interviews. I am still interviewing with several of these companies; four positions were filled with internal candidates; two positions were downgraded; and two positions were filled by executives with more closely related industry experience. This opportunity with your organization appears to be an

ideal match with my industry background and professional qualifications. Wouldn't you agree?"

Interview Success Strategy:
Explain the wise and deliberate use of your time since your last position.

With this type of response, you are changing your interviewer's perception of you from someone who has searched unsuccessfully for over a year to someone who has devoted the time, energy, and resources necessary to plan and execute an effective and appropriate search campaign. No, you have not been in the market for 13 months; only for five. No, you are not desperate, but rather looking for the right opportunity.

Interview Challenge #5 –
It's Someone Else's Agenda

The one obstacle that you will never be able to overcome is someone else's agenda. There are so many factors beyond just you, your skills, qualifications, employment history, and interview performance that will impact whether or not you are offered an opportunity. Each company and each hiring executive have their own agenda, needs and expectations. Some of these you can influence; others are totally out of your control and you may never even be aware of them.

Consider the following as agenda issues that you cannot influence:

- Other candidates whose qualifications more closely match the company's needs.
- Other candidates whose industry experience more closely matches the company's needs.

- Other candidates whose network of contacts could be of more value to the company.

- The company's desire to hire a minority or woman, masking that behind the veil of interviewing every qualified applicant.

- Promotion of an internal candidate to the position.

- Elimination of the position through restructuring, downsizing, rightsizing, or another corporate initiative.

- The company's poor financial performance and inability to commit to another executive salary.

- The company's takeover through a merger, acquisition, LBO, or MBO.

- Recruitment and selection of a friend, past colleague or associate for the position.

Once you accept that there are things totally out of your control in the interview process, you will be better able to accept the loss and frustration you may feel when you are not offered an opportunity for which you thought yourself a perfect candidate. Sometimes it is best to just let it go, realizing that you cannot and never will be able to influence someone else's agenda, particularly when it is someone whom you most likely do not know.

Never a Negative Word

When responding to difficult questions like the ones above in Interview Challenges #1 through #4, it is imperative that you do not criticize your past employer, past supervisor, or co-workers. You must make every attempt possible to positively position your responses without dishonesty or misrepresentation. Remember that your challenge is to sell your success, your contributions, your value, and your track record of performance. It is okay to share the difficult situations and the not-so-pleasant facts. But be sure that you communicate in a positive manner and leave your interviewer with a favorable impression of you and your background. If you communicate a negative message about a past employer or supervisor, the result is a negative impression of you.

5

Winning Answers to Tough Interview Questions

TO BEST DEMONSTRATE HOW to respond to specific interview questions, this entire chapter will focus on a typical executive candidate and how he answers 50 sample interview questions, many of which are asked in virtually every interview; others that are less frequently addressed. His answers will provide you with an excellent overview of how and when to use traditional, situational, and/or behavioral responses to specific interview questions asked in all different types of interview situations. You can use this candidate's interview responses as strategic tools to help you develop your own winning answers to the many questions you will be asked.

Play to Win!

Our fictional job seeker, Edward J. Logan, is a 50-year-old senior executive, currently employed as the Executive Vice President of Business Operations with Broadcast Technology, Inc., an early-stage venture that he joined in 1997. Ed began his career with a Fortune 500 company (X-Technolabs, Inc.), advanced rapidly through a series of increasingly responsible sales and marketing management positions, transitioning into his senior management/general management role six years ago. He was downsized in 2001 as part of a company-wide workforce reduction. It was then that he accepted the opportunity with his current employer, believing that the market potential for their technology was significant.

Ed has broad experience across all core functional disciplines including strategic planning, new venture planning, finance, technology development, field operations, sales, marketing and national account management. His experience also includes, but to a lesser degree, human resource affairs, purchasing, facilities management, and community/corporate relations.

Ed has worked in start-up ventures, turnarounds, and high-growth organizations in both U.S. and international markets. He has been an active participant in due diligence reviews and financial negotiations for mergers, acquisitions, joint ventures, and other strategic partnerships.

Ed believes that his negotiation, communication, and interpersonal skills are what have propelled him throughout his career and been the driving force behind his success. Others have commented that Ed's greatest value is his consistent ability to deliver positive financial results, despite market conditions, regulatory challenges, and competitive forces. Ed has taken this comment and integrated it into his search strategy, believing that, although the humanistic characteristics of a strong business leader are vital, the bottom-line financial results will catch someone's attention.

To better understand the following responses, consider that Ed is currently interviewing for a position as the President of The Technology Team, Inc. (hereinafter referred to as TTT), a $75 million telecommunications company servicing the Northern California market. The company needs fresh ideas, a new market vision, and renewed energy to continue its growth and expansion throughout the national market.

Question #1
Tell me about yourself.

This question is one of the classics and there are two vastly differing schools of thought on how to best respond. Tradition tells us that what the interviewer is seeking is a brief summation of your career. As succinctly as possible, lead your interviewer through your career history with a brief mention of some of your most notable achievements.

Ed would say,

I began my career with X-Technolabs in 1984, was selected for the executive leadership development program after just two years, and earned eight other promotions during my tenure. My earliest experiences were in field marketing, sales, and regional management. In each position, I delivered strong revenue results. I was then promoted to the senior management team of a troubled business unit, working with two other executives to facilitate its turnaround. Once it was profitable, I left that unit and spent the next three years introducing internal change and organizational development programs throughout the corporation. The next several years were devoted to developing new ventures as our industry exploded. My final assignment was as General Manager of a $150 million business unit where

*not only did I deliver a 25% improvement in bottom-line profitabil-
ity, I helped to position the company as the #1 market leader in the
industry.*

*Currently, I am employed as the Executive Vice President with
Broadcast Technology. I joined the company in 2001 after a careful
review of their technology, proposed marketing strategy, and high
level of technical talent. My responsibilities are largely devoted to
providing strategic direction for both technology development and
market launch. To date, my team and I have closed over $45 million
in sales prior to full product roll-out. In addition, I have been an
active leader in developing the company's manufacturing and production processes, working with our plant management team to create a best-in-class organization with full ISO certification.*

The above is what would most likely be considered a traditional
response to the "Tell me about yourself" question. More modern
thought has, however, changed the strategy for answering this question. Instead of giving a career history that virtually reiterates what is
already on your resume and will be the foundation for the remainder
of the interview, use this question wisely and to your advantage.
Briefly, and with powerful words, summarize who you are today and
the value you bring to that organization. Your answer can incorpo-
rate results and experiences from your past, but should not simply
repeat what is on the resume. Keep the focus on the professional you
with some personal you mixed in as appropriate.

If Ed were to answer the "Tell me about yourself" question using
this strategic approach, he would state,

*I am a well-qualified, senior-level management executive who has
met the unique challenges of start-up, turnaround, and high-growth
companies. Never working in what one would consider a status-quo
organization, I have continually been challenged to deliver results
that required strong creative, strategic, and tactical leadership. Most
significantly, in each and every one of these situations, I have deliv-*

ered measurable financial improvements in revenue, market share, cost, and bottom-line profitability.

A few specific examples that best exemplify my performance include my current leadership of an early-stage technology venture for which I have generated $45 million in new revenues within one year. In my previous position as the General Manager of the Partners in Technology Division of X-Technolabs, my team and I not only improved profitability 25% but also positioned the company as #1 in the national market. Earlier career achievements were equally notable during my tenure in sales, marketing, turnaround management, and new venture development.

In summary, I consider myself a consummate management professional, confident in my ability to tackle virtually any challenge by assembling the right personnel, identifying the appropriate markets, and building product recognition despite competition. Of paramount importance to my success has been my ability to build relationships throughout all levels of an organization, defining common goals, implementing incentives and challenging my workforce to deliver their best.

With the above answer, you get a much clearer sense of Ed's value, energy, and results. The presentation is sharper, more aggressive, and on the executive level.

Now, on to Ed's answers to the remainder of the interview questions.

Question #2
How long have you been looking for a new position?

I launched my search several months ago, but very quietly and confidentially. Since then, I have been on about 10 interviews, making it to the final group in all but three. In fact, I was offered an opportunity with another emerging technology company but was extremely concerned about their long-term market potential so I declined the opportunity.

Because I am currently employed, and secure in my position for the immediate future, I do not feel the need to jump into another opportunity. Unless, of course, the opportunity is the right one for me and for the company.

Question #3
Why are you considering leaving your current position (applicable only if employed)?

Although I still believe that Broadcast Technology has great technological innovation and tremendous market potential, the investor group backing the company has decided to not invest any further funds in R&D or market development. As such, although the company has experienced strong growth over the past year, I anticipate the growth curve will ebb. As with any emerging venture, financial backing is critical to long-term development. Considering the circumstances, I have determined that it is best if I resign my position and look for opportunities elsewhere.

Let me just mention that neither the investor group nor the other members of the executive team are aware of my decision. I prefer to keep my search confidential until such time as I have received an offer. I am sure that you understand and appreciate my situation.

Question #4
What did you wish to accomplish in your current job but were unable to do? Why?

What I was unable to do in my current position was negotiate for additional funding from our investor group. The company is owned by a small venture capital firm which invests only in emerging technology companies. As a result of their narrow investment focus and the tremendous volatility within virtually all technology industries, they have suffered significant financial losses over the past few years.

Although Broadcast Technology delivered strong revenue results, the investors determined that they were not willing to increase our funding, no matter the long-term potential. The president of the company has not given up hope and is currently negotiating with two other investor groups who may have a potential interest in the company. However, the situation is now much too uncertain for me to remain.

Question #5
Why did you leave your last position?

I left my position with X-Technolabs because the company was no longer thriving. During my tenure we had experienced a long period of phenomenal growth in all of our core business units. The environment was dynamic and the results unprecedented in the industry. Unfortunately, in the early and mid 1990's, as the industry experienced tremendous competition, we found ourselves floundering. Our technologies were becoming outdated, many of our international joint ventures were experiencing financial difficulties, and our cash situation was at its worst ever. At that point the company felt the need to undergo massive internal change and reorganization. Over 35% of the entire workforce was downsized, including myself and more than 35 other senior managers and executives. Although I was sad to leave the company after so many years, the change afforded me the opportunity to again join a high-growth venture. I look back at my years with X-Technolabs with tremendous pride and personal satisfaction.

Question #6
What will your current (or most recent past) supervisor say about your performance?

Currently I report to the President of Broadcast Technology, who is not aware of my decision to seek a new career opportunity. As such,

I would ask you not to contact him at this point in time. Of course, if we come to a mutual agreement, I know that you will eventually want to speak with him.

What will he say about me? I believe that John will comment on my ability to provide vision and then translate that vision into specific action plans. He will tell you that one of my greatest contributions to the company has been my ability to build consensus and create a team-based environment. He will also mention the strength of my communication and negotiation skills, my ability to accurately assess the potential of proposed new ventures, and my involvement in controlling operating costs during a period of growth and expansion. Perhaps most significantly, he will substantiate the fact that my contributions were the catalyst for our strong revenue growth this past year.

Question #7
What will your colleagues say about you?

My colleagues will tell you that I know what I am doing, that I am able to quickly grasp control of a situation, make tough decisions, and move forward.

Question #8
How would your subordinates describe you?

I believe that the majority of individuals who have worked for me will tell you that I am honest, fair, and above board. I don't believe that there should be any secrets (other than proprietary financial, market, product, and/or technology information). As such, I think that my teams have felt they each contributed and that their efforts were noticed and appreciated. I believe that everyone wants to feel as though they are valued.

My employees will also tell you that I am a good listener. I value their opinions and am willing to take the time to hear what they have to say.

"Lastly, I think they will say that they had to work hard for me. I expect a lot from them, but am willing to give a lot in return."

Question #9
What did your most recent appraisal say about the quality of your work performance?

"My last performance review focused primarily on the financial results my team and I were able to deliver. As you are now aware, we increased revenues by $45 million within that year, improved our market share ratings, and initiated development of our next-generation technology.

"My review commented on the value of my leadership competencies, my success in providing a renewed corporate vision, and my performance in pulling the team together to deliver such results. Additional comments reflected my strong communication skills, interpersonal relations skills, and ability to evaluate proposed new ventures and accurately forecast their potential.

"Broadcast Technology ranks executive performance on a scale of 1-5 with 5 being outstanding. I received a rating of 5 on 27 of the 30 criteria; the remaining 3 were rated as 4."

Question #10
Have you ever been fired or resigned from a position?

"Fortunately, I have never been fired. But as we have discussed, I am considering resignation from my current position due to lack of investor funding to support continued growth, technology development, and international expansion."

Question #11
What is the greatest value you bring to this organization?

The greatest value I bring to TTT is my ability to deliver positive financial results. Most relevant to your organization has been my success in accelerating growth through new product development, new market development, sales training, and expansion into alternate distribution channels. As General Manager of X-Technolabs, I delivered 25% revenue growth within an intensely competitive market, improved our market share by 16%, and increased our national account base by more than 40%. More recently, with Broadcast Technology, I have provided the strategy and operating leadership that has increased our revenues by more than 100% in less than one year. Second-year projections forecast an additional 75% growth in the U.S. market with initial penetration into Latin American and European markets.

Note that Ed is using specific examples of his past job responsibilities to highlight his achievements as they directly relate to the needs of the company. In just five quick sentences, he was able to communicate action, results, success, and value.

Question #12
What are your immediate, 5-year, and 10-year goals – personally and professionally?

My current goals are focused on obtaining a new senior-executive opportunity within the technology industry. It is where I can be of most value and deliver the strongest results. The ideal position would entail a vast array of responsibilities, including P&L, strategic planning, new venture development, finance and budgeting, sales, marketing, and organizational development. From what I have learned about your company and your current search, I believe that this may be just the right opportunity for us both.

My goals for the next 5-10 years would include continued progression to executive positions of even greater financial, marketing, strategic, and operating responsibility. A company such as this would provide just the right environment to increase my leadership responsibilities as you continue to penetrate new markets, build new technologies, and expand your customer base. I believe that I can provide the energy, strategy, and tactical operating leadership critical to your profitable growth.

Question #13
Define your leadership and management style.

My leadership style is rooted in my belief that no organization is stronger than its workforce. To that end, I have worked tirelessly throughout my career to create working environments that encourage individual development, performance, and reward. If it were not for the commitment and effort of my staff, many of the successes I have achieved would never have been possible. Employees are the backbone of any successful organization. They are what keep it moving forward internally and what earns our reputation externally.

Creating team-based environments is one of my greatest strengths. I do not believe in the traditional hierarchy of 'them and us', realizing that each individual employee wants to believe that his/her contributions are core to the success of the company. As such, I have led numerous internal change and organizational development initiatives, all of which were focused on creating a proactive, team-based organization working collaboratively to achieve our goals, meet our challenges, and realize our vision.

As you take all of this into consideration, it is also important to remember that someone has to be the team leader, the key decision maker, and the impetus driving the organization forward. Although I am always dedicated to my workforce and strive to make them feel a part of our success, I do also appreciate that my role as team leader is equally significant. If the team does not have a primary voice, there is no direction. I have always been that voice, guiding each organization to success while nurturing and energizing the workforce.

Question #14
Define your decision-making style.

The word proactive perhaps best describes my decision-making style. Never daunted by challenge, I approach each business decision much like I would a puzzle, looking at each individual piece and then integrating them into one whole to see the entire picture.

I believe that no decision relies just on one piece of information. The internal and external factors influencing a company are much too complex. Effective decision making requires a thoughtful process to clearly and accurately analyze all factors which not only affect the decision today, but the long-term impact throughout the company.

I also believe that it is vital to encourage the participation and input of others within the organization. Certain decisions may be straightforward; others require greater contemplation during which the opinions and recommendations of my staffs and management teams have been essential.

Question #15
Define your success in problem solving.

Let me begin by stating that I attempt to view problems not as problems but as challenges and opportunities for positive change. With that in mind, let me discuss my tenure as one of three senior executives leading X-Technolabs's core technology division through a dramatic turnaround, revitalization and return to profitability.

For more than 10 years, the division had operated profitably, met its goals, launched revolutionary new technology, and estab-

lished itself as a market leader. More recently, it had faced escalating operating costs, a volatile marketplace, and instability within the workforce. Budgets were out of control, managers were not performing to plan, and financial results had plummeted.

Before making any decisions as to what course of action to take, I created a structured process to investigate the situation. I began with a comprehensive review of the organization, working to identify the specific issues that had so negatively impacted the organization. This required extensive research and communication with individuals throughout the entire company, an in-depth analysis of financial results, interactions with customers, communications with vendors, and a host of other research-based efforts. After I had obtained the preliminary data, my management team and I spent weeks analyzing, extrapolating, and interpreting the information, providing us with a clear picture of the factors negatively impacting performance.

Once the other executives and myself understood the situation, we were able to devise the strategies, introduce the business processes, and lead the internal change initiatives to regain control and reenergize operations. In summary, we not only achieved our turnaround objectives but exceeded them. Costs were cut by as much as 32% in the production area, sales productivity increased 28%, market share reached an all-time high and profitability was restored within the first year.

Based upon my success in uncovering the underlying issues impacting performance, I then spent the next several years working as an executive troubleshooter throughout numerous divisions, business units, joint ventures, and operations within X-Technolabs. Using the formula I had developed, I was able to quickly go into each organization, identify the core issues, implement new strategies, revitalize operations, and restore performance. I am particularly proud of my success in this role.

Question #16
Tell me about your communication skills.

Let me use this opportunity to highlight my communication skills as they relate to external corporate affairs with our customers, bankers, vendors, and financiers.

Maintaining relationships with customers was critical to both Broadcast Technology and X-Technolabs, just as it is to TTT. We are in a customer-driven industry where our name, our image, and our market perception are vital to our performance. Appreciating the tremendous influence our customers have, I have always made it a point to maintain an active communication channel throughout the customer base. This has included direct presentations and negotiations with national and other large accounts, as well as a quarterly newsletter I developed that is distributed to all customers throughout both U.S. and international markets. My sales and marketing management teams know that I am readily available to support their efforts, resolve problems, and provide whatever type of customer support or communication may be necessary to ensure quality service and retention.

In relation to my involvement in communicating with the banking community, I have always played an active role in establishing commercial banking, credit, and lending relationships. Working with the CFO of both companies, I participated in defining our immediate and long-term cash requirements, negotiating corporate lines of credit, and introducing strategic cash management tools. My value in these communications has not only been my knowledge of the business, the industry, and the market, but my strength in building relationships based on trust and integrity.

Vendors have been another audience with whom I have communicated, primarily related to price, performance, and quality. Most significantly, I assisted X-Technolabs's Manufacturing Manager in developing a process to enhance vendor communications, eliminate inaccuracies, and ensure that all parties were aware of the needs and expectations of the others. These types of efforts were particularly critical in supporting our new ventures and turnaround efforts.

In relation to our financiers, in my current position I communicate regularly with the venture capital firm funding our operations. Primarily this has included presentations regarding the company's financial status and formal requests for additional funding. The latter has been quite similar to what is commonly referred to as roadshow presentations, outlining our current operations, use of funds, and forecasted results. Again, my ability to communicate openly and honestly has been a catalyst in nurturing these relationships.

Question #17
Tell me about your negotiation skills.

To best exemplify my negotiating skills, I want to tell you about a new venture I developed while working for X-Technolabs.

In 1989, I realized that the opportunity for expansion into European markets was emerging. To capitalize upon that opportunity, I researched potential joint venture partners in the UK, France, Germany, and Spain. After months of investigation and preliminary discussions, I determined that the most advantageous opportunity would be a co-marketing agreement with a French-based technology company.

The negotiations for this venture were intense. X-Technolabs had its objectives, and while the French company was also motivated by the potential financial rewards of this venture, they had their own priorities. To achieve consensus, I assembled the three top decision makers from each organization for an entire week of negotiations. During this time, we addressed each and every issue impacting our agreement, redefined our strategy, realigned our field coverage, and outlined new areas of responsibility. All financial con-

siderations were closely addressed until we reached agreement. On day four, the deal was closed. We then spent day five touring local sites and getting to know each other better. Over the first two years the partnership generated $180 million in revenues, well beyond the best of anyone's expectations.

Question #18
Are you computer literate?

Yes, I have excellent computer skills and am proficient with Word, Excel, and PowerPoint. Of course, I am not a programmer or systems analyst, but I have worked closely with senior-level IT staff throughout my career to translate our business needs into technology applications. Let me also mention that I am extremely Internet and email literate.

Question #19
What is the greatest contributor to your success?

As I have previously mentioned, I believe that the most vital contributors to my personal success are my communication, interpersonal, mentoring, coaching, and team-building skills. Earlier in our discussion, I outlined my commitment to developing and nurturing my workforce, believing that they are the foundation for any company's success. Of course the vision, energy, and leadership style of the executive team is just as critical. However, without the support of each and every employee to achieving that vision and meeting organizational goals, there would be no success. It is through their daily efforts and contributions that performance, financial, operating, and strategic objectives are met, if not exceeded.

I learned quite early in my career that if I was successful in building top-performing teams, not only did we achieve our objectives, but our perception in the marketplace would be strong. As such, I have devoted my energies to creating organizations with

*open channels of communication across all levels and have been suc-
cessful in integrating mentoring, employee-development, and team-
building programs. The results of these efforts are clearly supported
when you review the financial performance of each organization
under my leadership.*

Question #20
How do you deal with stressful situations?

*I take a step back and take a deep breath! In fact, I sometimes think
that I am the poster child for stressful situations – aggressive start-
up ventures, high-growth companies, operating-unit turnarounds,
and other performance-driven situations. Each of these involved
different stresses, but the ultimate goal for each was improved revenue and profit performance. And, yes, I felt the stress to perform –
stress from the board of directors, shareholders, executive management teams, and operating management teams. Schedules were often demanding, budgets were tight, and goals were aggressive.*

*However, stress is only as intense as you allow it to be. Over
the years I've learned to look at these situations objectively and not
allow myself to get caught up in the tension and anxiety. It has been
critical that, as the leader of these organizations, I am able to maintain my composure, make good decisions, and continue to move
forward. To accomplish this requires effective skills not only in stress
management, but in problem solving, decision making, consensus
building, and organizational leadership.*

Question #21
What is the #1 achievement of your career?

*My most notable achievement occurred early on in my career as
Regional Sales and Marketing Manager for X-Technolabs's Mid-
Atlantic region. During my two-year tenure in this position, I was
able to increase regional revenues by more than 100%, capture over*

500 new corporate accounts, achieve dominant market positioning, and virtually eliminate competitive threats.

Now, when you look at my more recent achievements you may think that they have been grander. And perhaps they have. However, this early success gave me the confidence in myself, my skills, and my performance that has propelled my career thereafter. I would have to say that, on a personal note, this achievement was the most vital to my long-term career success.

Question #22
What are the top five contributions you have made during your career?

We have probably already covered some of this information in our earlier discussion, so I will briefly highlight what I consider to be my most valuable contributions and achievements.

- *$45 million revenue growth in one year for Broadcast Technology.*
- *Successful turnaround and return to profitability of X-Technolabs's core operating division.*
- *Negotiation and development of eight joint ventures in the U.S., Europe, and Latin America on behalf of X-Technolabs, a step that was vital in expanding the company's presence throughout both U.S. and international markets.*
- *Road-show presentations that raised over $200 million in venture capital and institutional funds to finance development of X-Technolabs's next-generation technology.*
- *Strong and steady revenue, market share, and profit improvements I delivered early in my field sales and marketing management career.*

Question #23
What are your greatest strengths?

My strengths are reflected by strong financial results and my ability to build, energize, develop, and lead top-performing teams. It's the money and the people.

Question #24
What are your weaknesses?

I believe my greatest weakness is impatience, wanting results today, not six months down the road. When I accept a new assignment, I am energized and immediately ready to move forward. However, over the years, I have learned to temper this enthusiasm with the realization that progress takes time, money, energy, and dedication. Success does not come overnight.

I might also comment that over time I have learned to place reasonable expectations on my staff. Early in my career, I believed that everyone should work 70 hours a week and make the job their life, just like I did. However, I can now appreciate the fact that although my employees work hard and give a lot of themselves, they are not 'married' to their jobs. They do have lives beyond work and I must respect that. Don't worry though; I still expect them to give 110% every day.

Question #25
What motivates you to perform and excel?

Challenge has always been my #1 motivator. When I look back at my college years, I can see it then. On the track team for four years, each year I set a goal for myself to improve my time. And each year I exceeded the goal because I was internally motivated and self-challenged to deliver. That part of my personality continues to thrive today and is evidenced by my success in leading new technology

*ventures through growth, expansion, internal change, and perfor-
mance improvement. The personal pride I feel when I have met my
goals is enormous and will continue to drive my performance for
the rest of my life.*

Question #26
Do you consider yourself a leader or a follower?

*I am definitely a leader, but a participative leader. I thrive on the
challenges of leading organizations and people, but also know that I
do not have all the answers. As such, I have always maintained a
cooperative working environment, valuing the ideas, recommendations and contributions of others – my management teams, my professional staffs, and my hourly personnel. Ultimately, however, one
person has to make the decisions and be accountable. I have worked
to place myself in that leadership position since early in my career,
and even as far back as high school and college. I was class president in my junior and senior years at the University of Missouri,
was team captain of both my high school and college golf teams,
and was active in leading various community sponsored events.*

Question #27
Are you a risk taker?

*I am a calculated risk taker. Before moving forward on any project,
I attempt to collect as much information as possible to ensure that
my decisions are based on fact and evidence, and not gut reaction.
However, I also realize that those who are not aggressive in moving
forward often do not win. I believe that a certain risk level is necessary for any executive to effectively lead a high-growth, high-per-
formance organization.*

Question #28
How do you determine or evaluate success?

I believe that success can be measured in two distinct ways: first, by bottom-line financial results and second, by personal pride and satisfaction.

Question #29
What is the worst mistake you ever made on the job and how did you remedy the situation?

The single worst mistake of my career was in 1994 when, as Regional Sales Manager, I ordered the production of 5,000 printed circuit boards for a new customer. Doesn't sound so bad, does it? However, I ordered production prior to the client's signature on the contract. I was young and the client assured me that he wanted the product. I was anxious to please, so I moved forward. Four days later, the client informed me that he had found a better price and was not interested in my products any longer. Even after all these years, I can still remember how I felt that day. The wind had been knocked out of my sails. I went home devastated.

Two days later I was renewed. I knew that I had 5,000 PCBs to sell immediately and I set out to find a new customer. Over the next three weeks, I knocked on more doors than I had ever done, negotiated aggressive incentive programs with my distributors and never gave up. I found a new buyer who not only purchased the 5,000, but ordered an additional 10,000 over the next year.

Needless to say, I have never again launched production until the contract has been signed.

Question #30
What have you learned from your mistakes?

Perhaps the greatest lesson I have learned is accountability. If I make a mistake, I must assume responsibility. As I have progressed throughout my career to positions of significant decision-making authority, I've taken the glory and the pats on the back. But I have also learned to take responsibility when results have not been what we anticipated or mistakes have been costly. As the business leader, no matter who in my organization makes a decision, I must ultimately accept the responsibility.

Question #31
If you could change something about your life, what would it be and why?

If we're talking on a professional level, I would have returned to college and earned my MBA degree. Although I do not believe it would make me any more qualified than I am now, the classroom is always a dynamic environment from which we can all glean new information, concepts, strategies, and tools.

Question #32
What are your views on continuing education? For yourself? For your employees?

Continuing education is vital, particularly in an industry such as ours that is so rapidly evolving. To that end, I have made a point of devoting time and energy to continuing my education. This includes attendance at more than 400 hours of training over the past 10 years, including graduation from Harvard's Executive MBA Program and attendance at the Center for Creative Leadership. Much of my continuing education has focused on further developing my managerial, leadership, communication, negotiation, and strategic planning skills. In addition, I have taken several short courses to improve my hands-on computer skills.

In reference to my employees, I also consider continuing education vital to both their personal and professional development. I actively encourage their enrollment in training programs and col-

lege courses and, when appropriate, am more than willing to absorb the training costs.

Further, I have justified development of numerous in-house training programs to provide the entire workforce with the opportunity for skills development. The results of these efforts have been a more motivated, more qualified, and more committed workforce who also understands and appreciates the value of continuing education to their current positions and long-term career goals.

Question #33
Who was your most valuable mentor and why?

The single greatest influence on my career was a gentleman named Ted Smith. He was my first supervisor when I joined X-Technolabs. As Ted was promoted, so was I, giving us the opportunity to work together for more than five years.

Ted taught me and nurtured me, adding to my responsibilities as I was ready, giving me new challenges to spark my performance, and always being available to support, guide, and mentor me. I believe that Ted's guidance accelerated the pace of my career development and growth. The valuable lessons he taught will be with me throughout my career and my life.

Question #34
When you are hiring, what do you look for as the most important attribute in a candidate?

By far, the single most important characteristic of any individual's success is attitude. Although I firmly believe that an individual must have the basic skills to perform the function, attitude is vital. An individual must want the position, have a positive attitude, be willing to learn, and have strong interpersonal skills. If someone has the basic qualifications, I can teach the job and fine-tune the skills. However, I cannot change attitude.

Question #35
Have you ever had a supervisor you did not get along with and how did you manage the relationship?

Early in my career, I worked for a gentleman who had been with the company for over 30 years. As Director of Field Sales, he was fully accountable for the profitable performance of the entire sales organization. I was one of his regional managers, responsible for the Midwest territory, including both commercial and government accounts. The first day we met it was evident that there would be conflict. I was eager to accelerate growth within my region, full of new ideas and energy, and ready to tackle the world. My manager, on the other hand, was extremely cautious, content with the status quo and not anxious to make waves during his last two years with the company. Every time I approached him with a new concept or new marketing strategy, he listened but was quite resistant to change. As hard as I pushed to launch some of my ideas, he stood firm.

Fortunately, both of us realized that we would be working together for two years and that we must find some common ground. At my urging, he and I agreed to an informal meeting outside of the office where we would both be comfortable in discussing our situation. We spent hours together that night, learned a great deal about each other and did find our common ground. I appreciated his situation; he learned to appreciate my talent and drive. Together, over the next two years, we further developed my region, realized a 32% increase in sales revenues, and were both commended by the executive team for our performance.

This was a most valuable lesson, teaching me that in virtually any circumstance, individuals can find common ground upon which to build.

Question #36

Have you ever had to fire someone for poor performance? If so, how did you manage the situation?

When I assumed leadership responsibility for the turnaround of X-Technolabs's core operating division, I was faced with a difficult situation. The individual who was responsible for the entire production planning, scheduling, and materials management function had not been performing to plan. His previous manager had discussed this with him on numerous occasions and clearly documented all their discussions. New plans had been devised and new processes had been developed, but nothing was ever implemented. Further, it was clearly evident that his mismanagement of these functions had a negative impact throughout the entire organization, was a primary cause for budget excesses, and had been the leading contributor to poor product quality.

I took immediate action, informing this individual that if his performance did not measurably improve over the next 30 days, he would be let go. Each week, for the following four weeks, I met with him to discuss his progress and provide my support. Still no effort and no results. Therefore, I did terminate his employment after 30 days and promoted an individual from within to assume his position. Subsequently, over the next six months, our budgets were back in line, quality had been improved by better than 85%, and we were well on our way to recovery.

This experience was difficult for me. In the past, if I had individuals who were not meeting expectations, I was always able to work with them to enhance their work performance. This particular individual was not willing to make any changes, accept constructive criticism, or work with other members of the team. I had no alternative but to let him go.

Question #37
What are you looking for in a new opportunity?

Challenge and the opportunity to make a difference are my two primary objectives in looking for a new executive opportunity. One thing that has always distinguished my career has been the opportunity to participate in a diversity of functions, projects, new ventures, and turnarounds. Each position has had its own set of challenges to be met, ranging from negotiating strategic alliances and joint ventures to redesigning manufacturing processes and cost structures, and everything in between. This is what has been my motivator – the chance to make a difference.

It is a similar type of opportunity that I am currently seeking. I know myself well enough to know that I would not be content with the status quo. I want the chance to help a company grow and prosper. And I would be proud to have the opportunity to work with you in achieving just that for TTT.

Question #38
How would you describe your ideal position?

I have probably described my ideal position in what I have just told you. Let me also mention, however, that I am seeking a position that will afford me a great deal of responsibility and decision-making authority. I am accustomed to that level of accountability and look forward to continuing as one of several top executives of an organization. I would also anticipate having either direct and/or joint profit and loss responsibility.

I want to be at the helm of an organization and be one of the individuals accountable for its growth and strong financial performance. The personal satisfaction I derive is what continues to move my professional career forward.

Question #39
What other positions are you interviewing for?

Currently, I am actively interviewing for two very different positions – one as General Manager of a small, yet well-established and financially solid telecommunications manufacturing firm. I have interviewed twice with this company and am scheduled for a third interview in two weeks.

The other position I am actively interviewing for is as Executive Vice President of Sales and Marketing for a Fortune 100 technology company. I had a brief conversation with the COO of the company last week and he was quite interested in my experience in new venture development. Yesterday, I spoke with his secretary to coordinate my travel arrangements and will be meeting with him early next month.

Both positions require an experienced senior executive capable of defining a new strategic direction, assembling the resources, and building market presence to drive revenue growth. In fact, virtually all the positions I have investigated – whether general management or executive-level sales management – have focused on companies seeking to grow and expand either in U.S. and/or international markets.

Question #40
What criteria are you using to evaluate the different companies you are interviewing with?

I would have to say that the primary criterion is the company's opportunity – its products, technologies, and market potential. I want to align myself with an organization that is moving forward, growing, and expanding. Of course, the financial stability of the organization is also quite important, but often there are inherent risks in taking advantage of new business opportunities.

I would be amiss if I didn't also mention compensation. Of course, I am looking for an opportunity where my compensation – whether it be salary, bonus, incentive, and/or equity – is commensurate with the energy, drive, and results I will deliver. Each of us wants to be acknowledged for our efforts and our contributions.

Question #41
Is job security a prime consideration for you?

This is a particularly tricky question to answer. Consider the fact that companies want to hire individuals who are committed to the organization, its growth, and its success. However, you must counterbalance that with the undeniable fact that today's corporate employment market is volatile and ever changing. The long-term security once offered by large corporations has, to a large degree, disappeared over the past decade. Companies don't want to adopt you; they want you to come in, fill an immediate need, and remain as long as the opportunity exists – a year, three years or 10. Situations change and you must be flexible.

Ed would respond with,

Of course, job security is a consideration. But perhaps more important is the opportunity and the challenge that it offers. I know that no company can ensure an executive of a long tenure in an employment market that is so volatile. Technologies are changing rapidly and companies must respond to this change. As such, a company's needs often change over time. Would I like to think that I might remain with TTT for five years, 10 years, or more? Of course. However, I am realistic in my expectations and know that things can suddenly and unexpectedly change after just a few years. I have accepted that as part of my executive career and am willing to take whatever risks are associated if the opportunity for success and reward exist.

Question #42
How long do you expect to stay with our company?

I would hope that this opportunity with TTT would be long-term as the company continues to grow and expand. To be perfectly honest, I am not particularly interested in accepting an opportunity that is anticipated to last only for a year or two. I am hoping to find an opportunity where I can be of value and contribute for years and years to come. Obviously, however, this will depend not only on my personal success, but the success of the entire organization.

Question #43
Suppose we were to offer you the position of President of TTT. If you could have only two other executives working with you to build this company, what would those individuals be responsible for and why?

I would have a Chief Financial Officer and a Human Resource Executive. I believe that the former is critical to any corporation. In order for me to perform my functions as the President or CEO of an organization, I need to know the financial facts and anticipated outcomes. The information and knowledge that the CFO provides is vital in plotting the best course of action.

Equally essential is the Director of HR. Although a great part of my career has been invested in developing my workforce, mentoring them, coaching them, and energizing them, I am not an HR Executive. I do not administer benefits and compensation; I do not develop HR information systems, and I have not been responsible for HR regulatory affairs. However, these functions are essential and require the skills of a specialist.

If you combine the expertise of these two individuals with my strong general management, leadership, marketing and organizational development skills, you would indeed have a winning executive team at TTT.

Question #44
What will you bring to this position that another candidate will not?

Not familiar with the other candidates that you are interviewing for this position, I would comment that the four greatest assets I bring to TTT are:

- *My ability to see the entire picture and how each functional discipline impacts the whole organization.*
- *My ability to consistently, and despite market conditions, deliver strong financial results.*
- *My energy, drive, and dedication.*
- *My in-depth knowledge of, and experience in, the industry. With over 20 years in technology, I know the players, the markets, and the technologies. This information and these contacts will inevitably provide TTT with a strong competitive advantage.*

Question #45
Are you willing to travel? How often?

Yes, I am more than willing to travel as may be required. Throughout my career, I have been in a position where travel was a necessary part of the job. This has included travel to customer sites, company operating locations, and new ventures in both the U.S. and abroad.

In the past, I have traveled as much as 35% of my time. More recently, it has been approximately 15%. That percentage of travel is acceptable. However, I do understand that there may be times when my travel schedule would be more demanding as new ventures evolve, new markets are penetrated, and new partners are brought aboard.

Question #46
What is your expectation for number of hours to be worked each week?

I would anticipate, at least initially, that I would be working a minimum of 70 hours per week. Perhaps more. None of my positions over the past 10 years have required less than an average of 55 hours per week; sometimes as much as 80+ hours if we were working on a particularly time-sensitive project or new initiative. I hope that I have already displayed my willingness to work hard, my initiative, and my commitment. That commitment extends to include whatever time may be necessary to plot our course, develop our business, and achieve the board's financial objectives. I am not afraid of hard work and not intimidated by long hours. Success requires effort and perseverance.

Question #47
Why are you interested in our company?

When this question is posed, you had better know the answer! There are many resources available to find information about the company you will be interviewing with. Call for an annual report, search the Internet, visit your local library, or make some phone calls. People want to hire people who know about them, not just have simply heard about them. Be sure that you are well prepared, have learned about the history of the company and its current operations, products, services, and/or technologies. An educated job seeker is always a winner!

Ed would respond with,

I am well aware of the success of TTT. I have always made it a point of knowing my competition, the major players in the industry and the early stage ventures that are poised to make a real impact – just like TTT.

My interest in TTT is for precisely that reason. Aware of the quality of your technology and the widespread impact it has already had in the industry, I know that the company will continue to grow, expand, and prosper. And I want to work for a winner. In researching TTT, I have also learned that your goals include international expansion into the Latin American and European markets, both of which I have had direct experience with. Further, I am acquainted with several of the members of your board of directors, individuals I worked with and/or negotiated with during my career with X-Technolabs.

TTT is definitely poised for dramatic growth and I am confident in my abilities to lead the organization to achieve your current goals and long-term objectives.

Question #48
What type of person would you hire for this position?

If the hiring decision was mine, I would outline the following characteristics for the 'ideal' hire. They would include the ability to see the big picture and deliver strong financial results, possess a high level of energy and drive, and have a wealth of industry knowledge.

Obviously, you are telling your interviewer that you would hire someone with precisely your qualifications without being quite so blatant with your statement. If you refer to the question that addressed 'What you would bring to this position that another candidate would not?', you will note that Ed's answer to this question directly mirrors his own strengths, attributes, and qualifications.

Question #49
Why should we hire you?

This is a critical question that allows you to succinctly and aggressively summarize your qualifications. Very often it will be asked as one of the last questions in an interview. If it is not asked by the end of the interview, it is your responsibility to introduce the topic. If the interview is coming to a close, you should end your presentation with, "Let me tell you why you should offer me this opportunity." Then proceed with your answer, which should summarize your core qualifications and experience as they pertain directly to that position.

Ed ends his interview with,

You should offer me this opportunity because I am extremely well qualified and believe that I have demonstrated to you my ability to deliver financial results within competitive new ventures and high-growth companies. Further, I have an excellent knowledge of, and network in, the technology industry, relationships that have been of value throughout my career and will continue to be critical in opening new markets, funding new ventures, and driving the development of revolutionary new technologies.

I bring to this position all the key management and leadership qualifications you require – strategic planning and business direction, technology development, multi-site operating management, P&L management, marketing, sales, capital raising, public relations, venture partner relations, team building, and organizational development. These have been the backbone of my success to date and will continue to move my career forward as I continue to advance.

One last point that I would like to leave you with is something that we have already discussed – my people skills. I can tell just from the short amount of time I have spent with you that you are also quite committed to your employees and appreciate their value and contributions. That is precisely the type of environment I am seeking…a company where people are the foundation, technology is the market catalyst, and positive results are the norm. This is certainly the perception I have gotten of TTT during this interview session.

Question #50
What are your compensation requirements?

This is perhaps the most difficult of all questions to answer and requires more than just a paragraph or single-page discussion of the topic. How do you negotiate an equitable compensation package, preferably larger than that which you are currently earning or earned in your most recent position without pricing yourself out of the running? How can you favorably negotiate incentives, stock options, and an equity interest? What about signing bonuses and benefits?

Compensation negotiations can be the most challenging and daunting task of any interview. For a comprehensive discussion of this topic, refer to Chapter 6, "Negotiating Winning Compensation Plans."

The Forbidden Fruit

Illegal Questions

In 1964, Title VII of the Civil Rights Acts was passed, making discrimination on the basis of race, sex, religion, or national origin illegal in personnel hiring, promotion, and decision making. Most interviewers are aware of these restrictions and will not ask illegal questions. If they do, generally it is because of their ignorance of the law.

Typical illegal questions include:

How old are you?
How many years until you retire?
Where were you born?
Where were your parents born?
What is your ancestry or lineage?
What is your race?
What is your native language?
Do you hold citizenship in any other country?
Are you married, divorced, separated, or single?

Are you living with anyone?

Do you have children? Are they in day care?

How much do you weigh? How tall are you?

What color are your eyes? Your hair?

Have you ever legally changed your name?

What is your maiden name?

What is your political affiliation?

What is your religious affiliation?

What holidays do you celebrate?

Do you belong to any social or political groups?

What is your medical history?

Do you have any disabilities? What are they?

How does your disability affect your performance?

Have you ever filed a worker's compensation claim?

Have you ever been arrested?

Do you have a history of substance abuse?

Do you have a history of alcohol abuse?

What medications do you currently take?

What does your spouse think about your career?

Where does your spouse work?

Are you the primary wage earner for your family?

What are the names of your closest relatives?

Was your military discharge honorable?

What is your credit history?

Have you ever declared bankruptcy?

Have your wages ever been garnished?

If your interviewer asks these questions, you have two alternatives. You can bring to the interviewer's attention that the question is illegal and refuse to answer it. However, at that point, you will most likely alienate the interviewer and close the door on the potential opportunity. If you are really interested in the position, you may chose to answer the question, despite its illegality. Think carefully about your response so as not to provide any information that would exclude you from consideration. Then, make a mental note that once you have accepted the position, you will attempt to positively influence the hiring practices of the organization to meet all regulatory and legal requirements.

On rare occasions, an interviewer may ask these questions only to see your response and how well you manage a stressful situation. Although this tactic is considered unethical as well as illegal, you should remain cool and even-tempered. You might inquire as to what relevance that question has to the position under discussion or use the opportunity to provide personal information that you believe is in your best interest. For example, if your interviewer inquires about your age, you may choose to give a straightforward answer. "I know that you are not allowed by law to ask that question, but I would be pleased to answer. I am 53 years old, in excellent condition, an avid golfer and tennis enthusiast, and just passed my last physical exam with flying colors."

With that answer, you have informed your interviewer that you are aware of the illegality of the question, but are quite interested in the position and willing to provide whatever type of information may be required. The interviewer should take the hint and steer clear of any further questions of that nature. Take the time, in advance, to think carefully about these illegal questions and what your responses will be if they are brought up in an interview.

Questions You Should Ask

As we have discussed earlier, interviewing is a two-way street. Not only will the interviewer have a prepared list of questions for you, you should also have given serious consideration to what information you want from the company. This is a time for you to gather information so that you can make an informed decision.

Review the following questions and determine which are appropriate for each particular interview.

- What are the duties and responsibilities of this position?
- To whom will I report?
- Where does this position fit into the organization?
- What are the supervisory, managerial, and leadership responsibilities of the position?
- Why is the incumbent leaving this position?
- What type of qualities would your ideal candidate bring to the position and to your organization?
- What type of experience and qualifications are you seeking in a candidate?
- What problems might I expect to encounter in relation to job function and personnel?
- May I speak with present and past employees to get their feedback?
- How long have you been with the company?
- How long has the President/CEO been with the company? What about other members of the executive team?
- What is the greatest challenge that the company faces today?
- What are the company's one-, five-, and 10-year plans?
- Why is this position so critical to the company's immediate and long-term success?
- Tell me about advancement and promotional opportunities.
- What is the salary, bonus, and compensation for this position?

There will probably be other questions that you want to ask, based on the particular opportunity and company under consideration. Be sure to jot these questions down prior to the interview, rather than trying to remember them all while you're in the actual interview session. The more prepared you are and the more intelligent the questions you ask, the stronger your interviewer's perception of you and your qualifications will be.

6

Negotiating Winning Compensation Plans

N
EGOTIATING COMPENSATION can be the single
most difficult component of your executive job search
campaign. How can you negotiate a higher salary than
that which you are currently earning without push-
ing yourself out of the running? How can you determine your worth
to a specific organization? Have you ever considered a lower salary in exchange for an equity interest? What is the cumulative

value of the benefits the company has to offer? Is the company willing to pay for performance and results?

There are so many considerations in negotiating an equitable compensation package and each must be addressed individually. It is imperative that you remember that the compensation package you negotiate today will impact your future earnings for years and years to come. A good rule of thumb if you are currently employed is that you can expect a salary averaging 10% to 15% over your current earnings.

Salary discussions can be extremely awkward. Your goal is to negotiate the best compensation possible. Your interviewer's goal is to control hiring and compensation costs. Immediately, there is disparity between the two objectives, which can lead to disparity in your negotiations. It is vital that you remember that most positions do not have a predetermined salary level and that most employers are flexible and willing to negotiate a fair compensation package to attract the right talent to their organization. Although their objective may be to control costs, their primary objective is a successful executive hire.

Executive job search candidates must remember that compensation is generally NOT a discussion addressed in the first interview. The objective of the first interview is to determine whether or not you have the qualifications for the position. It is a time that you and the company "get to know each other," allowing the interviewer to assess whether or not you have the professional qualifications, personal characteristics, attitude, and behavior they are seeking in a qualified candidate. Compensation discussions are usually, although not always, reserved for further in the interview process – perhaps interview #2, #3, or even #4.

It is very difficult to discuss compensation prior to a full understanding of the responsibilities and accountabilities of the position for which you are interviewing. If your interviewer does bring up compensation during interview #1, you might consider asking to delay that conversation until such time as you have learned more about the position and the company. About 50% of the time, the interviewer will agree; the other 50%, he/she will push you for an answer.

Prior to a salary discussion, you should have done your home-work. What do other companies in the same industry or market pay executives in this type of position? What do national salary surveys indicate? What are other executives in the company being compen-sated? The latter may be more difficult to determine if the company is not publicly held and compensation is privileged information. The more information you can amass, the better equipped you will be to negoti-ate a favorable compensation package.

Compensation discussions often begin with the interviewer ask-ing you, *"What are your salary requirements?"* One of the best strate-gies to deploy at this point is to respond with, *"What was the salary range you had in mind?"* This pushes the onus back onto the inter-viewer to at least give you some indication of what they expect to pay an executive in this position. The interviewer may respond with, *"The range we are willing to consider is $95,000 to $125,000."* Obviously, your answer is always, *"The high end of the range is certainly in line with my expectations."* The only time that this answer would not be appropri-ate would be if the compensation was significantly lower than what you are currently making, had recently made, or were anticipating for the position.

If you know that you will be replacing someone currently in the position (they are retiring, have accepted a new opportunity, have been promoted, or have been dismissed), you might ask, *"What is the incumbent currently being compensated?"* Again, the onus is back on the interviewer to give you some idea of what the salary may be.

If, however, your interviewer is not able to or willing to share the above information with you, you must then respond with specific in-formation regarding your requirements. The best strategy at this point is to mention your current or most recent compensation as a starting point. You might offer, *"In my current position as Vice President of Tech-*

nology, my base salary is $150,000 with an annual bonus ranging from $25,000 to $45,000. In addition, I have stock options, bringing my total compensation to just over $225,000 annually."

It is also recommended that you prepare a written statement of your current, or most recent, compensation package. Instead of simply stating that your current compensation package is $225,000, prepare a printed document that breaks down each component of your current package. You might include last year's versus this year's or this year's versus next year's compensation. This provides your interviewer with specific information that he/she can review and use as a baseline for the offer that they will be making to you.

When the salary topic is finally raised, and you have a more detailed understanding of the position, you will be better equipped to respond. Begin your answer with a brief summary of the position as you understand it:

"As I understand, the position of CIO will report directly to the President and be accountable for the strategic and tactical leadership of the entire information technology function. I will be responsible for a $32 million annual operating budget, a team of more than 200 individuals, and a direct management reporting staff of 10." A statement of this type clearly defines the level of position, financial accountability, supervisory responsibility, and value of the position to the company. It is a great point for leveraging favorable and financially rewarding compensation discussions.

Negotiating and Accepting the Offer

For executive job seekers, serious compensation discussions are generally delayed well into the interview process, close to the time or at the time the company is making you an offer. Unlike in your earlier positions, where salary was principally the only point of negotiation, executives must negotiate an entire compensation package that may include a combination of base salary, benefits, stock options, equity interest, signing bonus, performance bonus, and pension/retirement plan. Each point must be carefully evaluated and individually addressed.

When the time to discuss compensation finally does arrive, your best strategy is to listen carefully to what the interviewer is offering. Offers may be presented verbally, but are generally presented in writing. At this point, you have four basic options in response to the company's financial offer:

1. Accept it as it is presented and the negotiations are finalized.
2. Negotiate for additional compensation in the form of increased base salary, an equity interest, stock options, incentives, or an expanded benefits program.
3. Ask for time to think about the offer.
4. Turn the offer down, thank the interviewer for his/her time, and leave.

Options #1 and #4 are not recommended. With #1, you may appear too anxious and, in turn, too desperate. With #4, you have forever put yourself out of the running for the position.

Options #2 and #3 are your best strategy. With #2, you are demonstrating that you are an educated job seeker fully aware of your worth. Most companies expect that you will negotiate; it's part of the "executive job search game." Clearly state the specific areas that you would like the company to reconsider (e.g., base salary, signing bonus) and why you are worth more than they are offering. You can expect to negotiate key points back and forth until a mutually agreed-upon package is finalized. Remember, at this point, you are somewhat in control. The company wants you! Use that to your advantage without exploiting it. Be fair in your compensation requests, not outrageous. How you manage these negotiations will establish the precedent for how you will manage future negotiations with and on behalf of the company. This is the time to demonstrate your savvy, poise, professionalism, and determination. This is the time to show the company your ability to drive forward successful negotiations where both parties are satisfied and both parties are winners.

Option #3 is also an accepted practice. Once you have received an offer, you can ask your interviewer for a few days to consider it. Forty-eight hours is a normal time by which the company will most likely expect a response. Take this time to consider the compensation that has been offered, the potential for increased earnings, any other offers you have received or anticipate receiving, and all of the other particulars of the position. Will you be proud to be associated with the company? Were you impressed with the caliber of the other executives? Is the company's financial position solid? What is the company's reputation in the market? Will you be happy?

After you have considered all of the above, and any other relevant issues, contact the company and either accept the employment offer or initiate negotiations as in item #2 above. Just because you have asked for time to consider the offer does not mean that you must accept it exactly as it is presented. Remember, the higher the level of position, the more intricate the compensation package, and the more likely that negotiations will result.

Salary, Benefits, and Your Compensation Plan

As with any other business negotiation, your objective is to get the most you possibly can. Be sure that everything you agree on is clearly documented in your employment contract (see next section). You want to maximize your base salary, benefits package, bonus opportunity, and participation in company stock-related and deferred compensation programs. It is at this point where the information you have obtained relative to the compensation of the company's existing executive team will be of most value to you. And, despite all the conversation about your value to the organization and what a difference you will make, nothing demonstrates that more than when the pen hits the paper.

Base Salary

Base salary is almost always the #1 consideration when negotiating an equitable compensation package. If you are currently employed, you should expect a 10% to 15% increase over your existing base salary. This is also true if you have only recently left your last position. However, if you have been in the job search market for an extended period of time, this may not be the case. You will have to give serious consideration to the offer being made and not simply accept it out of desperation. Only you know your personal financial situation, and only you can make an appropriate decision.

In your employment contract, be sure that you are guaranteed *"a base salary of at least X with annual performance reviews."* In certain circumstances, base salary increases will be formally addressed in the interview, in the offer, and in your employment contract.

Employee Benefits

Traditional employee benefits are a vital component of every compensation plan. These will almost always include health, dental, disability and life insurance, and a pension or retirement plan. Also be sure to review the company's personal leave policy. These standard benefits are generally offered to ALL of the company's employees (albeit various options).

More recently, in an effort to attract qualified personnel and in response to underlying political currents, many companies have expanded their traditional benefit packages to include vision care, tax-free health care spending accounts, child day care, elder day care, and spousal life and disability insurance programs. Most of these are optional and will have an associated cost to you. Carefully review each offering to determine its relevance to your particular life situation.

Executive Benefits

After base salary, this is where you can MAKE THE MONEY! At the executive level, you can anticipate a combination of the following:

Bonus. Executive bonuses, just like those offered to other employees, should be based on your performance or the specific function or business unit for which you are accountable. Do not negotiate a bonus dependent upon the performance of an organization over which you have no control.

If you are currently in an employment situation where you are virtually guaranteed a bonus, make sure that you brought this to the attention of the hiring company during your initial compensation discussions. It is recommended that you negotiate a first-year guarantee to ensure that you will receive an equivalent performance bonus. If possible, negotiate a bonus of 10% to 30% over that which you would receive in your current position – another incentive to accept the new opportunity.

Signing Bonus. An attractive executive benefit is the signing bonus or one-time bonus. This can be used to cover your relocation costs (if appropriate) or as an incentive to lure you from your current position. Signing bonuses can vary widely in dollar value, from just a few thousand to tens of thousands of dollars depending upon the situation and your value to that company.

Stock Option Plans. These plans are widely used as employee incentives and/or part of an employee compensation package, and are usually reserved for the executives of a corporation. The executive is given an option to purchase the corporation's shares at a certain price (at or below the market price at the time the option is granted) for a specified period of time.

Stock option plans can vary widely from one organization to another, and often companies will have several plans operating simultaneously. They may include incentive stock options, nonqualified stock options, stock grants, stock appreciation rights, phantom stock options, stock purchase plans, and other alternatives.

Profit Sharing Plans. These plans are agreements that allow employees, generally executives, to share in a company's profits. Annual contributions are made by the company, when it has profits, to a profit sharing account for each executive, either in cash or through a deferred contribution plan (see below).

Deferred Compensation Plans. These types of plans are a means of supplementing an executive's retirement benefits by deferring a portion of his/her current earnings. Deferring income like this encourages employee loyalty and longevity. For these types of plans to qualify as a tax advantage, the IRS requires a written agreement between an executive and his employer stating the specified period of time for income deferral. This type of plan is irrevocable and must be made prior to the start of your employment.

Deferred Contribution Plans. These plans are negotiated arrangements in which an unused deduction (credit carryover) to a profit sharing plan can be added to a future contribution on a tax deductible basis. Deferred contributions can be taken as stock shares, bonds, or a cash equivalent. These plans are applicable only when an employer's contribution to the profit sharing plan is less than the annual 15% of an employee's total compensation as allowed by the Federal Tax Code.

Equity Participation. If you are offered a position as one of the top executives of a corporation, you may also be offered equity participation, an actual ownership interest in the company. If you believe that the company has significant financial potential, this can be an extremely rewarding benefit generally reserved exclusively for the "top team." Often this type of benefit is offered in what many may consider a high-risk situation. Just remember, high risk often translates into high reward. If the risk is such that you are willing to accept the position, then you should most likely be interested in equity participation. Be advised, however, that equity is often offered in exchange for dollars from your pocket. Only you can determine your level of comfort with this option.

Golden Parachute. These are a relatively new phenomena that have arisen as a result of the massive prevalence of corporate mergers, acquisitions, and takeovers. In theory, these plans are designed to "take care of you" if you are let go or demoted as a result of a corporate transition.

Golden parachutes can be golden! They will most likely include:

- One to five years of your highest base salary plus bonus annual compensation (your choice of lump sum or payment over time)
- Immediate vesting of, and access to, stock (you can either retain it as an investment or sell it back to the company at the "hopefully" inflated takeover price)
- Immediate vesting of pension benefits
- Immediate exercise of all options
- Immediate payment of all performance bonuses and incentives
- Continuation of company-paid medical and life insurance for the same duration as your compensation, or until such time as you accept a new position.

Golden Handcuffs. Be forewarned. There are also compensation programs that make it quite costly for you to leave the company. Certain options and incentive schemes require that you stay with the company for an extended period of time to get the benefit of what you are "earning" now. These types of programs are devised specifically to protect the employer – not the executive employee.

TAKE NOTE! If you are not well versed in stock options plans, deferred compensation plans, deferred contribution plans, pension plans, profit sharing plans, and other executive benefit programs, contact an attorney, accountant, or financial advisor who can help you evaluate your specific options. These are critical decisions that impact your immediate and long-term earnings, and should be carefully researched to make an educated decision.

In reference to the above discussion, consider that smaller companies, new ventures, and emerging enterprises may not be in a position to offer such a plethora of benefit programs. In this instance, you may be offered a higher base salary to compensate for the lack of benefits, or may be offered an attractive equity participation program when your efforts will have a direct impact upon the company's performance. This can be a potentially risky situation. Only you can determine your own "risk-to-reward" quotient that you can comfortably live with.

Executive Employment Contracts

We would all like to think that a verbal agreement and handshake are just as good as a written contract. They're not. To protect yourself and your family, you will want to get all of the terms of your employment and compensation in writing. Employment contracts, once a rarity, are increasingly becoming the norm, particularly for the executive job seeker.

Are employment contracts the same as offer letters? No, but they are quite similar. Both spell out the terms and conditions of your employment, your compensation package, and other relevant information. However, the more senior the position, the more complex the terms of the agreement and the more likely that not only will you receive an offer letter, but also an employment contract.

If you are provided only an offer letter, do not be alarmed. If problems, issues, or litigation arise between you and the employer, the offer letter will be invaluable in substantiating your claims (assuming your claims are valid based upon the specifics of your employment as stated in the offer letter). Be advised that you will almost always receive a formal offer letter. It is accepted business practice today.

> **WARNING!**
> Do not resign your current position until you have received, in writing, an offer from a new employer.

Assuming that you are being offered a very senior level opportunity, you can also expect to receive an employment contract which should include:

- length of the contract
- position title and reporting accountability
- your specific duties and responsibilities
- termination issues
- compensation package

The first issue, and one of the most significant, to be negotiated is the length of the employment contract. Your goal will most likely be a multi-year contract, guaranteeing employment for three years, five years, perhaps even longer. However, the agenda of the company will most likely be for a shorter period of time – generally one year. The employer wants to retain the freedom and flexibility to change the executive team as may be necessary due to market and economic conditions, competitive influences, financial obligations and liabilities, and other major factors impacting the company's performance and stability. In this situation, compromise is the key to agreement. You may have to decrease your expectations while the company increases their commitment.

If an employer wants to ensure your long-term tenure with the company, he/she may include an automatic renewal clause which can extend the contract indefinitely. It may be worded much like "This contract shall be extended for an additional three years unless either party notifies the other, in writing, at least six months prior to the termination of this agreement."

Your employment contract should not only include your job title and whom you will be reporting to, but also a detailed listing of all of your job responsibilities (much like a position description). Where will you be working? Will you be elected to the board of directors? Will you serve on the Management Committee? What are your bottom-line financial accountabilities? What functions, departments or organizations will report to you? Which employees will report to you? Be wary of phrases such as "duties as may be assigned" which are vague and open to vastly different interpretations.

Once in writing, this part of the document serves to clearly state what you are accountable for and to whom. If there is ever any question, both you and the employer can refer to this document to clarify any issues.

The fourth component of your employment contract is related to termination. Again, you and the employer will approach this negotiation with vastly differing agendas. Your objective is to agree to termination only for illegal acts or blatant negligence. On the other side of the table, the employer wants the flexibility to be able to terminate your employment for virtually any reason once the length of the contract has been fulfilled. In this situation, the employer will usually win. Generally, the only safeguard you will be able to negotiate is length of contract.

Your compensation package is the other most vital component of your employment contract. As discussed previously, it is imperative that every single component of your compensation be clearly documented in your contract. This may include base salary, performance and signing bonuses, stock options, pension plans, golden parachute plans, and other executive incentives.

Two other vital considerations in negotiating your employment contract are related to non-competitive and confidentiality issues. The employer wants to ensure that you will not be easily attracted to another company much like theirs (non-compete) and wants to protect their trade secrets, products, market intelligence, and other proprietary information (confidentiality).

When negotiating these elements of your employment contract, your objective is to make sure that they are fair to you. Obviously, the company is biased and will attempt to make these extremely restrictive and to their benefit. Not only may your non-compete agreement cover the length of your employment contract, it may extend for years beyond. Note that this can be a great bargaining tool for you. If you're so much in demand, the company will, of course, want to pay you dearly.

To protect yourself in a non-compete agreement, the first step is to try to eliminate it altogether. If that is not possible, it is advised that you negotiate the following:

- The clause is void if you are fired or your contract is not renewed.
- The clause prevents full-time work, not part-time consulting.
- The clause includes only companies that are in direct competition.

Be particularly careful in relation to the confidentiality clause. If the agreement is so pervasive and prevents you from discussing virtually anything about the company, it will be very easy to terminate you for the slightest mention of any information. Attempt to negotiate a contract that simply states "intentional disclosures that could be harmful to the company."

Both non-compete and confidentiality agreements are very difficult to legally enforce unless the company can demonstrate financial damage through loss of market share, loss of customers, loss of revenues, or loss of profits. However, there is an ethical issue here that cannot be overlooked. When you sign an employment contract in good faith, you are pledging your honesty and your loyalty to the company. It is "understood" that you should not take their trade secrets to a competitive organization, divulge privileged information, or share data regarding a pending patent. If you do, you are placing yourself in a potentially liable situation and may have to pay the consequences.

It is highly recommended that you consult legal counsel prior to signing an employment contract. The minimal cost of attorney's fees is well worth the expense. Not only are you protecting yourself, you are ensuring that the contract does state exactly what you understand has been negotiated. A wise job seeker uses all the appropriate resources. In this instance, an attorney is vital.

Summary

Just as you feel confident in your professional competencies, you must also learn to be a confident negotiator. Know your financial worth and clearly present that worth to your interviewer. There is no one who will advocate on your behalf; only you. Do not settle for less than you are worth, hoping that in a short while the company will come to understand and appreciate your value, and be willing to offer a more attractive compensation package at that time. What you negotiate today will be the foundation for your compensation with the company for years and years to come. It will also be the precedent for your future earnings.

Keep the following strategies, concepts, tips, and techniques in the forefront when the infamous salary negotiations arise.

- If at all possible, allow the interviewer to raise the topic of compensation; not you.

- Attempt to delay salary discussions until you are well into the interview process. If pushed, you can simply respond with the fact that your salary requirements are open, negotiable or flexible.

- An easy way for interviewers to screen out potential candidates is by raising the salary issue early in their discussions. This can be an extremely efficient strategy to eliminate potential candidates who are "overpriced."

- You must be able to clearly state why you are worth a specific salary or compensation package. This is best accomplished with specific examples of your past performance, level of responsibility, and notable achievements (as they directly relate to the company with which you are interviewing).

- If, in your original discussions with the company, you stated that your current compensation package was $145,000 per year, stand by that number throughout all of your negotiations. If, after four interviews and an offer, you comment that although your base was $145,000, you also received an annual bonus of approximately $35,000, negotiations will most likely come to an abrupt halt. Why? It is not necessarily because of the additional $35,000, but rather the fact that you misled the company in your initial discussions. More than likely, the offer will be rescinded.

- If an offer is made by one company and you are currently in the final interview stages with another company, contact the latter to let them know that you have received an offer. Give them the opportunity to make a counter-offer if they are able to reach a decision. This can only be to your professional and financial advantage.

- Always remember that the ultimate purpose of your interview is to demonstrate your worth to a prospective employer. Do not attempt to translate your worth into dollars until such time as you have been successful in communicating your value to that organization.

7

Winning Follow-Up Strategies

Once an interview has concluded, there are several courses of action that you must immediately follow to keep your name at the top of the list of qualified candidates and ensure that you are invited back for another interview and, eventually, are extended an offer. Devote the effort necessary to:

- produce powerful thank-you letters.
- Follow up on the telephone.
- put your contact network to work on your behalf.

Power Thank-You Letters

There are two types of thank-you letters – traditional letters and power letters. The former is what you probably think of when someone mentions a thank-you letter. It's a quick note acknowledging the time an interviewer spent with you and saying you look forward to meeting with them (or someone higher up in the organization) again.

Power thank-you letters are even better. They serve the same purpose as a traditional letter (a quick thank you), while providing you with the opportunity to again sell your product – you. They are harder hitting than a traditional letter, packed full of information you've selected to further sell yourself into the position at hand. Power letters have three distinct purposes:

1. To bring attention to the specific skills, qualifications, experiences and achievements you bring to the table that are directly related to the requirements of the position and the needs of the company. Think of your power thank-you letter as a second-stage marketing tool, highlighting the features and benefits of the product most attractive to that specific audience.

2. To overcome objections. The power thank-you letter is the ideal platform to discuss the company's concerns relative to your qualifications, background, knowledge, product expertise, industry experience, and more. Again, the letter is a tool that, when used wisely, can favorably present information and explain situations that may previously have been considered liabilities.

3. To ask for the next interview or then the job. If you have just finished your first interview with a company, write them a power thank-you letter that asks for the opportunity for a second interview. If, on the other hand, you've interviewed several times with the company, then it's time to ask for the job. If you don't ask, you may not get the opportunity!

ELENA MONTAGUE

9 North Green Street
Market Town, PA 19877
(215) 383-2522

October 7, 2004

Troy Bartlett, Jr.
President & CEO
SymTech Technologies, LLC
8700 Grand Boulevard
Austin, TX 77877

Dear Mr. Bartlett:

First of all, thank you. I thoroughly enjoyed the time I spent with you and your management team during my recent visit to AAA. The commitment that each of you has to your employees and, in turn, their commitment to the company are remarkably unusual and admirable in this age of constant corporate change and reorganization.

Yes, I want to be a part of the AAA management team as your new HR Director. What I've I learned over the years is to "not fix that which is not broken." In this regard, I am referring to the corporate culture you have created and which I believe has been the foundation for much of AAA's success. Therefore, it is not my intention to change that which already exists; rather, my goal is to nurture that culture and your employees to even greater heights of performance.

Although we have discussed the following HR issues, there are several key points I would like to address:

- **"Staff Up and Win"** is an aggressive but realistic goal to which I bring significant value. As the first HR executive with Peabody, I created the entire recruitment and selection process, bringing more than 100 employees into the company. With Lillihand, I spearheaded recruitment for operations in both the U.S. and Europe. For Baxter, I launched an initiative to recruit 450 professionals to our engineering organization.

- **Acquisition integration** is another area in which I have solid experience to support AAA's aggressive M&A program. Knowing the success of your existing organizational culture, I believe it is imperative that the individuals retained are completely assimilated into the existing culture, becoming viable and productive contributors within a relatively short period of time.

- **International business affairs and expansion** has been one of my key management responsibilities. Specifically, I directed international recruitment, staffing, and generalist HR affairs for more than 1000 expatriate and foreign national employees. I am sensitive and responsive to cultural differences and successful in optimizing those differences to strengthen overall performance.

The goals that AAA has outlined for the immediate and long-term growth of the company require strong HR leadership today. The optimum path is to bring a professional into the organization, assimilate them into the existing culture, and allow them to initiate the plans and actions to support profitable growth. I would like to be that individual, responsible for building the leadership and technical talent that will successfully lead AAA into the future.

I hope that this information is of interest to you and has further demonstrated my value to AAA. I look forward to continuing our discussion and interviewing with other members of your management team. Thank you.

Sincerely,

Elena Montague

Elena Montague

Power Thank-You Letter Designed to Overcome Objections

MICHAEL R. HENDERSON
1215 Marquis Manor Hwy

St. Louis, MO 64158
Home Phone: (619) 999-3333
Email: LRH356@earthlink.net

May 12, 2004

Lawrence Ramon
President
Quick Title Equity, Inc.
190 Wabash Avenue
Chicago, IL 66666

Dear Larry:

Since our meeting last Monday, I have given careful thought to our conversation and the tremendous market opportunities that are opening for Quick Title. I am fully confident that I will succeed in building a strong and successful business development team. Let me take just a moment to address a few key points.

First and foremost, I am a "dealmaker" and marketer, able to capture market opportunities and deliver strong revenue and asset performance. I tackle each new project with a two-pronged focus: (1) negotiate the best possible transaction that is truly a "win-win" for each partner; and (2) create strategic and tactical marketing programs that achieve a strong and sustainable competitive position.

We have spoken at length about my achievements in new business development, new ventures, asset management and asset growth. We have discussed my success in structuring and negotiating complex financial transactions, improving cash flow, and strengthening partner relationships. Enough talk; now it's time for action.

You're right. I have never worked in the Chicago market. However, I have demonstrated my ability to build presence in other markets nationwide (e.g., Minneapolis, St. Louis, Phoenix, Charlotte). Further, I have an extensive network of contacts across the country, many of whom are well connected in Chicago and are more than willing to introduce me around town.

I have always been fortunate. Networking is a natural process for me. I am able to quickly ascertain who it is that I must establish a relationship with, identify the appropriate channels to do so, and quickly begin the process. In turn, despite often unfamiliar territories and personalities, I have quickly established myself in key markets. I am not daunted by challenge, but, rather, motivated to succeed and beat the odds.

I hope that you and I have the opportunity to continue our discussions. Thank you again for your time and your support.

Sincerely,

Michael R. Henderson

Michael R. Henderson

Power Thank-You Letter Designed to Ask for the Next Interview

WILLIAM R. LENTZ, III
Bill_Lentz_III@yahoo.com
9889 Florida Avenue
Richmond, VA 22209
(804) 888-9372

July 22, 2004

Raymond Greenspun
President & CEO
Greenspun Industries, Inc.
22 Dell Highway, Suite 2009
Boca Raton, FL 38928

Dear Ray:

Thanks for the conversation and the interview. I've been searching "quietly" for a new position for several months and this is really the first assignment that has sparked my interest. Now, I'd like to take a few minutes to highlight my success in sales, marketing, and customer management as it relates to the position with your company.

As one of only four executives with SY-4 Technology, not only was I responsible for selling and marketing the company, its products, and its technologies, I was also one of the key drivers in the customer service/support organization. In addition, I was the lead contact for many major customers and am personally credited with closing over $200 million in sales with AOL, Federal Express, Siemens, and others.

My most significant contribution has been the recapture and resurrection of the General Electric account, now SY-4's largest and most profitable customer. To understand the impact of this achievement, we have to go back four years when GE was in the process of telling SY-4 it was going to change vendors (after a six-year relationship). They gave me a challenge and I delivered. I made an immediate (that afternoon) proposal to GE based on a new architecture which met all of their critical objectives. They traveled to another one of our locations, they believed in what I promised, and they bought. GE now generates over $80 million in revenues each year for the company.

Further demonstrating my performance in selling, marketing, negotiating, and closing has been my leadership of several mergers and acquisitions. Most notably, I finalized the sale of assets and intellectual property that was being negotiated by the new CEO. Negotiations had stalled and I was brought in. Under my leadership, we closed the deal and had a check in 72 hours, just in time to post positive financial results for year-end.

In closing, it is appropriate to point out that one of the keys of good selling is good listening. If you do not understand your clients' needs and expectations, the relationship will never grow and the partnership will never solidify. This is perhaps the greatest value I bring to any organization: my ability to "hear" what a customer is saying and respond with the "right" products, services, and support.

I'm excited about this opportunity and look forward to continuing our discussions at another interview. I await your immediate response.

Sincerely,

William R. Lentz

William R. Lentz III

Winning Telephone Follow-Up Strategies

If, after a specified period of time, you have not heard back from the company, it is recommended that you follow up with a telephone call. When you call will depend on when the interviewer said they would be in back in touch with you. If you were told you would be contacted within two weeks and two weeks have passed, pick up the phone and call. If no specific period of time was offered, wait two to three weeks and then call. The onus is on you to keep your name at the top of the list of qualified applicants, maintain visibility without being overbearing, and move your candidacy forward.

Then, use your time wisely on the telephone. Reiterate your interest in the position and the company, and briefly highlight one or two items about your experience that you feel are of most value to that organization. Tell them you want the position. Ask how they are proceeding in the interview process, if they have made any decisions, and when you can expect to hear from them. Tell them you would welcome the chance to meet with the executive team again and have the opportunity to further expand on your skills and qualifications. Consider this activity to be a marketing follow-up call. Be professional yet assertive in attempting to move the interviewing and hiring process forward.

Often it is quite difficult to get the person you wish to speak with on the telephone. It may be that individual is extremely busy and filling the position is not #1 on her list of priorities. It may be that the company is still actively recruiting and interviewing, and is not ready to offer anyone a second interview yet. Or, bottom line, the interviewer may be attempting to avoid you because, for whatever reason, you are no longer considered a primary candidate.

If you find that you are having difficulty getting the person you wish to speak with on the phone, feel free to leave one or two messages; no more. If you do not hear back from them, chances are likely that you are no longer in the running, that the company has decided not to hire, or any one of a number of other reasons. Continuing to try to get yourself back in the door for another interview can be futile and a total waste of your time, resources, and energy. Do not continue to call over and over. It will not do any good. If the company is not interested in you, that's it, and rarely, if ever, can you do anything to change the hiring committee's decision. Just let it go and move on to more promising opportunities.

Do not be surprised, however, if six weeks later, after no contact, you get a phone call to come in for another interview. Often the hiring process takes much longer than anyone would anticipate either because of time constraints, the number of qualified candidates, or other more critical projects and responsibilities facing the interviewer and the company. In the meantime, make sure that you have been aggressively continuing your job search with more networking, more ad responses, an expanded direct mailing effort, or new Internet postings. A comment from an interviewer stating that your qualifications look great and that you are indeed a top candidate really means nothing until such time that you have an offer letter in your hand. Always keep your search moving forward until you are sitting at your new desk in your new office.

Put Your Contact Network to Work on Your Behalf

If you were networked into or recommended for an interview, get in touch with your contact immediately after the interview. Tell him how the interview progressed, share interesting facts you learned about the company or the individual you interviewed with, and be honest about how you think things went. Most important, be enthusiastic and express your interest in the position and the company. Then, ask your contact if he would be willing to make a follow-up phone call on your behalf to see what the company's impressions were. Did they like you? Are they considering you? Are they going to offer you a second interview? Where did you stack up against the competition?

What were any potential objections to your candidacy? Ask your contact to "put in a good word" on your behalf. It can only work to your advantage.

This type of market intelligence can be invaluable in guiding your future communications and interviews with that company. Hopefully, your contact will get back to you quickly with specific information. Take the positive comments and work to further leverage and favorably exploit them with the company. When you write your power thank-you letter, make sure to mention the top one or two items your network contact mentioned to you that most impressed the company, and then highlight how your experience in those areas will translate into success for the company. Take any negative comments, think hard about your responses, and work to overcome those objections. Explain why they are not liabilities, but, rather, can be of value to the organization or can be transitioned into more favorable attributes.

If your contact is reluctant to phone the company, ask if he would be willing to write a quick note or email message. You'll still benefit from the "good word," albeit a bit more passively than a phone call. In this situation, you will not be able to wait until your contact gets back to you with information and ideas to work into your power thank-you letter. You'll have to move forward and hope that your insights are in line with the company's needs, expectations, and impression of you.

8

Tips From the Top

A
S WITH ANY TOPIC ABOUT job search – resumes, cover letters, Internet postings, salary negotiations, and more – there many, vastly differing opinions about how to effectively interview. Everyone involved in the business of job search (e.g., career coaches, career counselors, professional resume writers, outplacement consultants, university career development personnel) has different ideas, strategies, tools, and techniques for interview success. Each believes that his sugges-

tions and recommendations are the best and are vital to your success in today's competitive executive market.

Following are "Tips From the Top" – proven success strategies for proactively managing your interviews and positioning yourself as a top candidate. Carefully review and heed the recommendations of these individuals – HR executives, outplacement consultants, recruiters, resume writers, career coaches, and others – for each has earned a reputation for excellence in interviewing and job search. It's an honor to share their suggestions with you.

To avoid repeating lengthy lists of professional credentials and certifications that each of these experts has earned, here is a quick summation:

CCM	Credentialed Career Master
CCMC	Certified Career Management Coach
CEIP	Certified Employment Interview Professional
CPRW	Certified Professional Resume Writer
JCTC	Job & Career Transition Coach
MRW	Master Resume Writer
NCCC	Nationally Certified Career Counselor
NCRW	Nationally Certified Resume Writer

The Executive Mindset for High-Stakes Success

Deborah Wile Dib, CCM, CCMC, NCRW, CPRW, CEIP, JCTC, and President of Executive Power Coach and Advantage Resumes of New York, tells us:

> Today's new executive job interview is a high-stakes exercise with a high-gain outcome. It is fraught with equal parts of peril and reward for the company, the interviewer and the interviewee. All parties are looking for 'the best skill fit' (translate, 100%+ fit), with the 'best chemistry' at the 'best price', all combined within one person and package.

How do executives face the massive challenge of out-distancing the competition and creating employer desire for their skills and abilities? The following four essential steps will help executives master the new executive interview and out-compete in the new executive marketplace.

Step One: Reframing perception

Today's executive must bring to the interview process the same intensity and 'failure-is-not-an-option' mentality that he brings to his most mission-critical projects.

Today's executive must mentally reframe the interview to become a mission-critical business meeting between peers rather than an interview between decision-maker and applicant.

Step Two: Information gathering and interpretation

Today's executive must see the interview as a top-level, high-ticket sales call or a high-stakes, critical-agenda board meeting. The success of such a meeting requires an intimate knowledge of the background and problems of both the hiring company and the executive.

Gathering comprehensive background information on companies is by no means easy, but it is crucial to success, and it is no more difficult than the executive's toughest tasks on the job. This background information is foundational to the executive's ability to present himself as an essential resource who can meet and surpass goals, solve problems, position the organization for growth, manage change, and create shareholder value, among many other skills.

Step Three: Building the case for employment

Once such information is known, the executive must dig deep to identify and discover the brand-defining, solution-proving accomplishments that will irresistibly illustrate his ability to overcome the organization's challenges and that will powerfully predict additional success. Savvy executives will have completed this exercise far ahead of the interview by understanding and building their personal brand and keeping an ongoing record of their career-defining and brand-building accomplishments.

An executive who has branded himself correctly will have mapped his brand to his target market and, through visibility-building, radar-screen activities, will be a known quantity consistently sought by companies and recruiters for top positions. This visibility positioning will have the executive 'pre-sold' before entering the interview.

Step Four: Building chemistry and doing the job

Step four is the 'deal maker', the thing that compels the decision-maker or board of directors to present an offer. Step four requires drawing upon the 'peer-to-peer business meeting' concept to control the interview—to suggest brainstorming problems right in the interview (and possibly in other business locations of the facility, depending on the job that needs doing).

Brainstorming between peers allows the decision-maker to work with the executive, as he would do on the job, as part of the management team. Brainstorming allows the executive's 'chemistry component', that indefinable energy field so intrinsic to the hiring process, to become real. Brainstorming allows the executive's problem solving to shine and creates desire for those solutions (and desire for the solutions' provider!). Brainstorming showcases the executive's ability to think on his feet and develop workable ideas. Brainstorming predicts future success. Brainstorming is doing the job to get the job.

Doing the job to get the job allows the executive to manage and shine in the many types of interviews he will encounter during the hiring process and negates the need for extensive memorization of interview responses.

By understanding the organization, by knowing his personal brand and his abilities, and by bringing his skills, integrity, and authenticity to each interview meeting – in short by 'behaving his way into the job' – today's executive will be prepared for the challenges of today's high-stakes interviews and create a win-win hire for himself and for his target company.

It's All About Chemistry

Kent Black, an Executive Career Consultant in San Rafael, California, former Group Vice President with Drake Beam Morin, and former Senior Vice President with J. Walter Thompson, says:

Creating rapport and identifying common background are critical to establishing a strong connection during senior-level interviewing. Such a foundation, combined with the ability to comfortably align one's principles to those of the corporation, are the basic requirements for a mutually successful interview at the senior level.

As in all interviewing, it is important to be well versed in the needs of the interviewer and the company as well as being prepared to extol your skills and abilities, particularly as they relate to positioning yourself as the best candidate for the job. However, interviewees at the senior level frequently have comparable skills, experience, and functional abilities. Therefore, it is the ability to create a connection to the personality of the interviewer and the culture of the company that will determine who is selected.

It is well documented that good interpersonal skills are absolutely mandatory in the senior-executive ranks and are often more important than any particular technical or functional set of skills. Extensive research done by the Center for Creative Learning and the Manchester Group found that 40% of senior-executive new hires fail within 18 months, principally because of the executives' lack of ability to effectively manage direct reports or relate well with peers. The inability to manage the boss and function in a politically savvy way came in second in the ranking of reasons why the relationships failed. Failure to meet objectives was a comparatively weak third in this ranking.

Here are the most critical factors in establishing interviewer rapport and winning opportunities:

Common Ground – If you have background, interests, or history that the interviewer can easily relate to, it is amazing how quickly formalities and barriers melt, and an aura of openness in communications is established. For example, if you were born in the same area, or went to the same school, or share similar work experiences or interests in sports and hobbies, or have volunteered time to causes and charities that have similar purposes, a commonality is established that creates a more relaxed and friendly atmosphere. A positive rapport will pave the way for an effective interview experience. Be sure to cover these bases in your answer to the almost always asked question, 'Tell me about yourself'.

Compatible Chemistry – Evaluate how you relate to the people you interview with and/or just meet in the interview process. Are these people with whom you would like to spend time, not only on the job but also socially? Recognize that not all will or have to pass the social criteria, but it is a good place to start your assessment. If there is no one you would like to socialize with, then you are probably in the wrong company.

Cultural Fit – Are you in agreement with the company's values, mission statement, overall purpose, and future direction? What can you find out or what do you know about their history in this very important area? Does this company 'walk the talk' or are these conviction-driven principles either non-existent or only for show? If your due diligence reveals a good 'fit' with the beliefs and values most important to you, then the likelihood of a successful connection with this company is increased.

The issue of whether you 'can do' or have the 'will to do' the job, while obviously important, is often not as significant as how well you 'fit' the culture of the organization.

Put Yourself "In the Zone"

Jay Block, JCTC, CPRW, in West Palm Beach, Florida, talks to us about interviewing in the zone:

Truth be known, effective interviewing is nothing more than effective communication. And it's as much about delivery style as it is about content. Here's a key phrase to write down: Interviewing in the zone is not only about what you know, but how you feel about what you know. In other words, you need to be prepared for the questions – yes. But you need to deliver your message with confidence, purpose, and passion.

When athletes are about to perform, what are they thinking about? Are football players studying their playbook before they come out on the field? Are skaters and gymnasts studying their routines before a big performance? No! Peak performing athletes prepare by getting in the zone – mentally! In fact, most coaches will tell you that gold-medal performances require no thinking at all. Performance time is not the time to think – it's the time to become 'instinctively engaged'.

A young cocky kid named Cassius Clay climbed in the ring in 1964 and against all odds beat the mighty Sonny Liston. Both were prepared physically, but Cassius Clay fought 'in the zone'. You see Clay, who later changed his name to Mohammed Ali, became the 'greatest' because he successfully blended the mental and physical. In fact, more times than not, he psyched out his opponents. And I'm sure you can think of times when the underdog – the team or person with the least talent – won. Why? Because talent without emotional engagement is wasted energy.

What does all of this have to do with interviewing for a job? Interviewing is no less a performance than a sporting event. Interviewing is no less a performance than opening night on Broadway. Interviewing is no less a performance than a presidential debate. Remember the debate between Kennedy and Nixon? Nixon won according to the few who listened to the debate on radio, but lost in the eyes of the masses who watched it on television. Why? Apparently, Nixon's content was better than Kennedy's, but his physical delivery was inferior. To excel in the interview – to interview in the zone – you have to be well prepared with your material. But more importantly, you must deliver it with energy, enthusiasm, passion, and confidence.

"Study communications at any major university and you'll discover communications are comprised of three basic components: (1) Physiology (55%), (2) Tonality (37%), and (3) Language (7%). So, when you prepare for an interview, if you spend 90% of your time rehearsing answers to tough questions, understand that you have invested 90% of your time on something that only makes 7% of the difference. We are told that first impressions are important – dress, proper grooming, a firm handshake, eye contact, a warm smile, and so on. Now you know exactly why! Because 55% of all communications is physiology. Physical impressions linger long after the words are forgotten.

Now remember when our parents told us that it's not what we say, but how we say it? Listen to a speech delivered by a presenter in a monotone voice – and chances are you'll fall asleep. Listen to that same speech delivered by Robin Williams or Whoopi Goldberg, and they'll keep you sitting on the edge of your seat. The lesson here is clear. In order to interview in the zone, you must demonstrate emotion and passion. This doesn't mean you have to be a 'Type A' personality and bounce off the walls. What this does mean is that you fully connect with your interviewers, build rapport, and communicate in a way that gets them excited about you and your value to their organization. I advise my clients to listen to their favorite music before an interview – to do whatever they have to do to 'pump themselves up' and to perform at their emotional best. Most people don't interview well because they just don't feel emotionally well going into the interview. They're nervous, uncomfortable, and uncertain. Uncertainty is a recipe for disaster. Confidence and control are the keys to success.

In summary, there is no substitute for preparation. Know the company you're interviewing with. Be prepared to answer these two questions at the beginning of the interview: (1) What do you know about our company and why do you want to work for us? (2) What are your skills and qualifications and how do you see them contributing to our organization? Prepare for the tough questions, for sure. But spend more time preparing your delivery. In the end, there are '3 P's' that allow you to interview in the zone: Preparation, Purpose, and Passion. Prepare with a clear purpose – and be sure there is passion, energy, and enthusiasm in your delivery. That will separate you from the competition. Then your only problem will be choosing which job offer to accept!

Research 101 For Every Candidate

Beverly Harvey, a CCMC, CPRW, CCM, and principal of Beverly Harvey Resume & Career Services in Pierson, Florida, works with senior executives worldwide and advises:

Step one in preparing for a successful interview is research – extensive research! Be sure you have gathered sufficient information about the company so that you can promote the benefits the company will derive from hiring you. Research the company to learn as much as possible about its products and services, its missions and goals, and how you can help the company achieve its objectives.

Researching the Company. Begin by visiting the company's website. Review the marketing strategy to see how the company positions itself in the marketplace. Study the company's products and services. Look for its annual report, company history, officers' and directors' bios, mission statements, press releases, subsidiaries, strategic partners, and customer list. Also, look at its career or employment section, and review the job listings and job descriptions to get a sense of its hierarchal structure and corporate culture.

If a company does not post press releases on its website, you can search for press releases at MediaFinder.com (http://www.mediafinder. com) or various newsfeeds such as:

- **PR Newswire** (http://www.prnewswire.com)
- **Business Wire** (http://businesswire.com)
- **Dow Jones Newswire** (http://www.djnewswires.com/)
- **CBS Market Watch-News** (http://cbs.marketwatch.com/news)
- **NPR** (http://www.npr.org/)
- **Reuters** (http://www.reuters.com/)
- **Bloomberg** (http://www.bloomberg.com/)

Researching a Public Company. For additional information about a company's financial status, the following websites will provide you with the company's SEC filings, quarterly and annual reports, and other information:

- **Hoovers Inc.** (http://www.hoovers.com/)
- **Thomas Register** (http://www.thomasregister.com/)
- **SEC/EDGAR** (http://www.secinfo.com/)
- **Wright Investor's Service** (http://www.corporateinformation.com)
- **LexisNexis** (http://www.lexis-nexis.com)
- **KnowX.com** (http://www.knowx.com/)
- **D&B** (http://smallbusiness.dnb.com/) or (http://www.dnbmdd.com/mddi/)
- **Thomson Research** (http://research.thomsonib.com/)

To find out more about a company's corporate culture and what it's like to work for the company, conduct a search at:

- **Vault.com** (http://www.vault.com)
- **Wetfeet.com** (http://www.wetfeet.com)

Researching a Private Company. Because private companies are not required to file financial information with the SEC, it can be difficult to find in-depth information about them. Companies are required to file with the Secretary of State in the state where they are established. Select a state from the pull-down menu on the Secretary of State website (http://www.nass.org/sos/sos.html) and you will be directed to that state's website, where you can search for information about a particular company.

A few other resources for researching private companies include:

- The Forbes Top 500 Private Companies (http://www.forbes.com/tool/toolbox/private500/)
- INC. 500 - The Fastest Growing (Private) Companies In America (http://www.inc.com/home/)

- D&B (http://smallbusiness.dnb.com/) or (http://www.dnbmdd.com/mddi/).
- Thomas Register (http://www.thomasregister.com/)
- Dow Jones, VentureWire (http://www.venturewire.com/)
- Freedonia (http://www.freedoniagroup.com/private.html)
- Ward's Business Directory of U.S. Private and Public Companies published by Gale and available at libraries.

Researching 'Inside' the Company. Now that you are armed with everything you could find out about the company through its website and outside sources, call the company. Start with a customer service representative and a sales representative. Let her know that you have a "meeting" scheduled with Mr./Ms. _____, and that you are gathering information for the meeting. Ask her about the company's products and services and request sales literature. Ask her about the company's target market, what makes its products and services unique, why customers purchase the products/services, and what types of problems customer service representatives resolve.

Before hanging up, ask the representative who else you should speak to in the organization. Ask the representative for the name and number of a department manager who can provide additional information. When calling the department manager, use the representative's name and ask questions appropriate for that person's area of responsibility. Again, let her know that you have a "meeting" scheduled with Mr./Ms. _____, and that you are gathering information for the meeting. At the conclusion of the conversation, ask for the name of another manager in the organization. Keep repeating this process to learn as much as possible about the organization.

While speaking with individuals in the organization, find out the names of the company's vendors and competitors. Give them a call as well. Ask the vendors about the products and services they sell to the company. Ask the competitors how their products and services are different and solicit feedback regarding the company that will be interviewing you.

The Interview. Present and demonstrate your strengths, expertise, and value proposition. Ask the hiring decision maker, what are the company's most pressing problems that they would like you to resolve. Based on your research, knowledge, and experience, communicate the specific contributions you can make immediately and in the future.

Through your research, you will be able to convey your knowledge of the industry, company, products, and services during your interview. This will instantaneously position you above the other candidates and clearly demonstrate that you are interested in, and qualified for, the position. Being well-versed and well-prepared will allow you to consistently perform at your best.

Is the Company Right for You?

Don Orlando, MBA, CPRW, JCTC, CCM, CCMC, of The McLean Group in Montgomery, AL, shared his insights:

Among the many obstacles facing you in landing that $100,000+ job is the age-old 'folklore' surrounding the hiring process. Among the most durable bits of this misinformation is the idea that the interview is really an interrogation run by a highly trained interviewer and designed solely for the purpose of seeing if you are 'good enough to join our team.' Forget that, for I'm going to give you the real story so that you can transform this necessary part of hiring into something you may use to your advantage.

Let's start with a powerful fact: When you are invited for an interview, the organization has qualified you for the job. (Sometimes companies interview people they have no intention of hiring, but that doesn't happen too often.) Now, let's dig a little deeper to see what that fact means to the interviewer and how you can use that information to help you find the right job.

Here's the good news: The interviewer is probably more nervous about the hiring process than you will ever be. After all, she had to convince her boss that the expense of hiring a new executive would be more than offset by the new or increased revenue that person would bring in. Beyond the need to deliver on her return on investment promise to her boss, several facts worry our interviewer. Like you, she sees people who aren't good in their jobs. And she knows that someone much like her chose those individuals as the best in a field of eligibles. She also knows that if she makes the wrong hiring decision, the mission won't get done and morale will suffer. Finally, if the bad hire has to be let go, her boss knows that disgruntled former employees are now attractive to their competition. They have proprietary information and knowledge of customer databases. Plus, the cost of hiring the wrong person can rapidly rise above $10,000. Finally, to make things worse, the interviewer doesn't hire often enough to be well trained for the process. That's why you will often read about the top 10 (or is it 20?) interview questions. Such lists tell you that interviewers are using a script and not focusing on finding the match between your unique excellence and their unique needs.

Let's make the interview more successful for both of you. Your goal is simple: have the interviewer tell you what his company's most pressing need is. Notice that we're not asking him to recite the responsibilities of the new job; you both know what those are. Consider the example of someone seeking to be a VP for Marketing. He can use his marketing skills in almost any industry. As he approaches companies, however, he may find very different needs. Company A, for example, may be rolling out a new product not associated with their existing line. Company B might market based on value and now faces competition marketing on price. If our applicant can get the company to tell him which problem is most important, many benefits accrue on both sides. The applicant can tell if this is a job he wants to do. The interviewer sees someone interested enough to ask the right questions. The resulting discussion will document how good a match this applicant is for the company and vice versa.

Notice that I've introduced the idea that you should evaluate the company. If you ask what their most pressing problem is and the interviewer can't answer the question, then Orlando's First Law of Employment is at work: Everything you see and everything you hear is condoned or encouraged by the leadership – without exception. In this case, someone (tacitly) approved assigning an interviewer to make an important decision without all the needed information. In other words, if the interviewer (an employee) doesn't know corporate priorities, how are you, the applicant, supposed to know?

You can get even more information about how good a fit a potential job is by asking questions like this one: 'Which observable behaviors will you use to judge my success?' You are not asking for a list of traits. Being 'hard-working and self-starting with strong communication and problem-solving skills' is great, for they are all useful, important things – which happen to define the minimum requirements for almost any job. No, what you want to know is which actions you can take on the job that will get you noticed and respected as a successful addition to the corporate team. Speaking of success, you will also want to be sure you're going to have all the tools you need. So why not ask about them with a question like this: 'Which resources, including decision-making authority, will I have under my control?'

Always remember that your goal and your interviewer's goal are the same: to collaborate to produce results benefiting both you and the company. You have taken time to be ready to talk about what you can offer. You want to be sure the interview (and by extension the company) has put the same effort into this project.

Be Sure You're "On the Same Page!"

George Crosby, President of the HR Network in Coopersville, Michigan, and former Vice President of Human Resources for Inryco, Inc., shares the following story.

Yeah…I spent nearly two hours with the search consultant who seems like a pro. She's presenting a final slate of candidates to their new CFO within the next two weeks. We really hit it off so I'm sure I'm going to meet him.'

He received a standard two-paragraph letter a month later, thanking him for his interest and lauding the credentials of the 'uniquely well-qualified executive' the client selected.

The guy had sized everything up perfectly, except the outcome. The search consultant did indeed like him a great deal. Nevertheless, when she made the call she decided he was not what her client wanted.

This little fiction is a composite of scores of experiences of executive job seekers. In it, the candidate let himself get carried away by the chemistry he and the search consultant developed.

No deception was intended by the consultant. She liked the guy and let it show, but made no allusions to him as an ideal fit for this situation. He drew that conclusion on his own.

Top-flight search people try to leave a good taste in the mouth of any prospect. It's wise practice, just as it's wise not to substitute their own tastes for those of clients. In a very real sense the consultant is akin to a 'personal shopper', an advisor/counselor who ultimately respects every client's right to choose what he wants.

"Even the most experienced job hunters are vulnerable to committing a couple of deadly errors:

1. They get too 'up' about attractive jobs. It causes those wearying rides on an emotional roller coaster. Working or not, do your search calmly, seeing yourself as a 'Cool Hand Luke', with your natural enthusiasm, and disappointments, under firm control.

2. They overestimate the license of strong chemistry with consultants, hiring executives, etc. At a point they lapse into unguarded ease, behaving much too casually during interviews. Among other things, those interviews are professional behavior examinations. Lull yourself into relaxing too much and you run the risk of blowing what you want to portray…that you're a polished business executive."

The Company's Agenda

Margaret "Margy" Porter, Founder of Millennium Associates, an organizational development and business advisory practice in Cary, North Carolina, and past Vice President of Human Resources for Scotland Memorial Hospital, reminds us of some critical issues that interviewers, hiring managers, and companies must face. Keep these thoughts in mind in order to better understand and respond to the priorities of the hiring company.

Whether you are part of an organization or have joined the ranks of independent entrepreneurship, planning for the recruitment process is one of the most important activities you will ever do.

Optimal success for a line of business, or an entire organization, depends on fit of skills and values and the challenges of the job. When I have started the process to hire within an organization or select a contract colleague, one of the most critical tasks was clearly defining the criteria for the job – and the criteria changes over time. To hire most effectively, you must closely evaluate the vacancy you have now. It is not the same job you may have had several years ago (or even six months ago), and the criteria probably have changed accordingly. Changes in key positions also provide opportunities for re-thinking your current structure. Be your own devil's advocate. Should responsibilities be reordered to be more effective in your current competitive environment? In any case, evaluate the job and criteria in 'today's mode'.

Once you have the appropriate skill essentials in mind, create the advertising to attract the right candidates. Then, develop multiple questions to verify the skills you seek in the interview process. Questions must relate to both interpersonal/communication skills and task/technical skills. 'Fit' also includes values consistent with the organizational culture. For example, if you have an organization with a strong team orientation, a sharing of credit (versus individual contribution), and a predominance of 'stakeholder' problem-solving for decisions, it is imperative to have multiple questions to identify those traits and skills.

The bottom line is that a great deal of planning is required before you ever get to recruiting, interviewing, and selecting. Established criteria for the job frames the entire process. If you want positive and effective results, put your time in up front in preparation – the rest will then fall into place.

Step-By-Step to Interview Success

Kathryn Jordan, Ph.D., NCCC, from Radford University in Radford, Virginia, has these recommendations for a successful interview:

The conclusion of all of your 'pre-work' in your job search is the opportunity to interview for a position. The interview is the critical element in any successful career transition. It is in one-on-one contact, whether face-to-face or by telephone, that an employer and potential employee can determine the quality of the matching process for a particular position. Here are several proactive steps you can take to ensure interviewing success.

1. **Advance preparation is the 'secret' of interviewing.**
2. **In many ways, interviewing is an art form.** The more you practice, the better you will become. In the interview situation, practice can enhance your performance. This practice should extend to your answers to the interview questions and role playing the actual interviewing process.
3. **Complete extensive research about the employer.** Find out everything there is to learn about the organization. Try to take a 360-degree approach. Talk to former employees, organizations that compete with the company, customers, and others. Your goal is to find out not only what trends and products may be impacting the organization, but also to hear the 'insider's perspective' about the organization.
4. **Think through how your background fits into this workplace.** Do you have similar previous experiences? What skills do you bring

that could be useful in this environment? How does your previous training give you an advantage in this company? What can you do for the organization? How can you help them make money?

5. **Identify possible questions and/or objections they may have to your background.** Remember, the best defense is always a good offense. Practice your answers to their objections in advance with another listener. Does your answer make sense?

6. **Prepare all details.** 'The devil is always in the details' is never as true as in the interview situation. Do not leave anything to chance. For example, you need to think about directions and timing to get to the interview, background information on the people with whom you will be meeting, what to wear, to print extra copies of your resume, etc.

7. **Prepare some questions to ask about the position/ employer.** Do not ask about salary and benefits, hours, training, etc. However, you can ask things like: 'How will I be evaluated? What are you looking for in the ideal candidate to fill the position? What do you see in the future for the position?' Try to develop several critical questions that you want to have answered by any future employer and utilize those in every interview situation.

8. **Follow up immediately after the interview.** Send letters to everyone with whom you spoke. Your goal in your letter should be to either re-emphasize how you fit or recoup in any areas where you forgot something critical that may be to your advantage in the hiring decision.

Your Resume as Your Expert Interviewing Tool

Rebecca Stokes, a CPRW, JCTC, and President of The Advantage, Inc., an executive resume and career marketing firm working with clients worldwide from their headquarters in Lynchburg, Virginia, tells us:

Your resume is the most critical job-search tool you have. It is your first introduction to a prospective employer, providing them with information they need to determine whether or not you are a qualified candidate. It is also the only physical asset you have to leave behind at the end of an interview to remind a prospective employer of your key career successes. Resumes are designed to be used as a conversation piece, highlighting the challenges, objectives, and successes you have achieved throughout your career. If used appropriately, your resume can distinguish you from the crowd, positioning you as the #1 candidate for a highly regarded, top-paying position.

During face-to-face interviews, resumes are great presentation tools. If asked about a specific accomplishment or challenge, your resume can help to direct the conversation and allow you to demonstrate your value. Here is an example: You are interviewing for a Chief Operating Officer position with the potential to take over as the next President/CEO in two years. Your resume already highlights your experience as the #2 executive in several unique business environments. In further highlighting your experience you might say, 'I feel comfortable and uniquely qualified to foster a positive relationship as a contemporary and business partner to the President/CEO. In fact, in two of my previous assignments, while I was orchestrating turnaround, rapid growth, and market expansion initiatives, I was also being groomed for the top position. It was my responsibility to be both a coach and facilitator, influencing the operating infrastructure while still being careful not to create a bureaucracy or damage the existing corporate culture. Due to the tremendous success attained in such a short period of time, both corporations were subsequently acquired by leading competitors and opportunities for long-term career advancement were limited'.

In the case of a telephone interview, use your resume as an outline for answering the preliminary questions of an executive recruiter or human resources executive who will be screening you against other applicants. You will also find out the specific requirements for the position and can direct the interviewer's attention to your attributes as they directly relate to the position. You can reaffirm the breadth of your experience in core functional areas, highlighting specific industry or business cultures that are identical to the assignment, or further expand on your accomplishments.

Career Portfolios for Show & Tell

Kirsten Dixson, JCTC, CPRW, CEIP, is a Founding Partner in Brandego, LLC and a Reach Certified Personal Branding Strategist. Here's what she shared about nailing your interviews:

Resumes are often viewed skeptically these days and many sound all too similar. In fact, your interviewer may be thinking that you have overstated the claims on your resume and perhaps even stretched the truth a bit. In fact, it's estimated that 40 to 70 percent of all job seekers enhance their personal work histories, according to a May 2004 article in HR Magazine.

A much better tool for facilitating a successful interview is a career portfolio. Rather than telling your interviewer about a project or an achievement, show tangible proof of your performance — graphs, letters, articles, photos, work samples, etc.

You certainly don't want to take over the interview with your show-and-tell, so aim to have one piece of evidence for each of your three to five most notable career achievements. The examples that you feature should also demonstrate your top strengths as relevant to your target position. In a face-to-face interview, be prepared to reference your evidence as it comes up in the conversation with physical samples or a printed version of your Web-based career portfolio.

Web-based career portfolios are ideal for both in-person and remote interviews since they can be viewed by anyone with Internet access and can feature video and audio as well. Imagine how easy it will be to show your work when you have a telephone interview. To get interviews, you can use your Web portfolio to differentiate yourself from your competition by including the URL in your emails to job search contacts and on your networking cards. If your portfolio is well executed, prospective employers will have the opportunity to see your unique value and supporting evidence before meeting with you in person. Your meetings can then become more productive by focusing on your qualifications in the context of the position.

A professionally developed (and it really should be) online portfolio will also be vital when your prospective employer 'Googles' you before the interview. Yes, Google has become a verb to many, so you had better be prepared. If you Google yourself, does your online identity reflect what you want it to say about who you are and what you have done? Foster the consistency of your personal brand by controlling what is found online about you.

Now that a conventional job may last only a few years and work is increasingly outsourced, it's also important to utilize a Web career portfolio as an ongoing career-management platform and not just a job search tool. If you regularly update it, you will be instantly ready for any future opportunity.

Credible Stories to Share

Louise Kursmark, CPRW, JCTC, CEIP, CCM, MRW, is the author of 11 books on careers, employment, and job search, including the soon-to-be-released *How to Find the Right Person for the Right Job Every Time* (co-written with Lori Davila). Louise offers the following advice:

Look for every opportunity to add credible stories and examples to your interview responses. Even when asked a situational ('What would you do…') or traditional ('What are your strengths?') question, you can answer the question and then add, 'Let me give you an example'. Stories are powerful and memorable and will set you apart from other candidates.

Here's an example of this strategy in action.

QUESTION: 'How do you feel about continuing education for your staff?'

STANDARD RESPONSE: 'I think it's absolutely critical to keep skills up to date to keep us on the competitive edge. As a manager, I always include training as a budget item and, in addition to formal programs, I look for other opportunities for staff education throughout the year. Often these are brief and inexpensive, but the knowledge my staff gains is invaluable. If you have a training mindset, you might be surprised what kinds of opportunities come your way'.

ADDED VALUE: 'Let me give you an example. When I was regional sales director in Ohio, my entire sales team spent at least a week in sales and product training every year. And we were consistently in the top 10 in the country. But I had a couple of people who struggled a bit keeping up to speed with our very technical products. Through my VP, I learned that a technical specialist from our number-one manufacturer was going to be spending two days with the reps in Kentucky, so I asked if two of my reps could join them. They spent the day learning about the latest product, got to ask all kinds of questions, and came away with a much more solid understanding of the product and its capabilities. In essence, they received nearly double the product training of the rest of my team. And it paid off. Sales for both of them shot up 10% that quarter, and both achieved their bonus every quarter that year for the first time ever'.

Notice how this example is presented using the simple-to-understand SAR (Situation-Action-Result) format, which makes it easy for the listener to understand the story and appreciate its value. Can you see how adding a specific example makes this candidate much more memorable than someone who stopped with the traditional answer? You can give yourself the same advantage. Mine your background to find numerous examples that support your key strengths. Jot down the situation, action, and result. Then, look for opportunities to add them to your interview responses, even if you are not asked specifically for an example. You'll find that these stories are a powerful weapon in your interview arsenal.

Great Questions to Ask Your Interviewer

Mark Berkowitz, NCCC, CPRW, JCTC, and President of Career Development Resources in Yorktown Heights, New York, shares some of the "pearls" he passes along to his clients.

(1) Typically, an interview may begin with the ubiquitous 'ice-breaker' question, 'So, tell me a little bit about yourself'. While this may seem, on the surface, to be a harmless question, the intent just might go considerably deeper. Oftentimes, the interviewer wants to 'scope out' a candidate and see what his priorities happen to be. Should the candidate relate which merit badges he earned in the Scouts or how his college major was selected, or should the candidate just plow right ahead and present the 'two-minute' pitch?

One tactic that gives the candidate an initial measure of confidence to get the interview off to a good start is to try and determine what the interviewer's hidden agenda is; what is most important to him. The strategy is to respond to the above-mentioned question as follows: 'I'd really love to. Where exactly would you like me to begin?' Now the interviewer must tip his hat and indicate a preference, which might just be, 'Oh, let's focus on your current position'.

No matter whether the candidate begins with his prepared two-minute pitch or receives an indicator as to what the interviewer is most interested in, I counsel them to bring to closure their opening presentation and 'tie everything up with a neat bow'. Candidates finish the presentation with something like this: 'And this brings me to why I'm here today. You see, with my experience and skills, it's obvious that a strong fit exists between what I bring to your organization and what you want or need from the person who is selected for this position'.

Frequently, my clients are somewhat apprehensive in contemplating certain types of questions which tend to fall into the category, of 'Gosh, I hope they don't ask me _____!' Fill in your own 'silver bullet' question(s). In most cases, these types of questions would reveal information that my clients feel portray weaknesses. I give them a homework assignment, asking them to write down three to five of the questions that they would hope to avoid. We then jointly work out strategies that portray these instances as potential strengths or indicators of 'unique selling features'. Even if these questions are never raised, the candidate goes into the interview with a psychological edge, prepared to demonstrate that he is highly qualified and no longer fearful of these types of questions. Being prepared really does pays off.

(3) If you don't know what the company's greatest concerns are, it is difficult to sell yourself as the answer to their needs. There are a number of successful strategies to get the interviewer to tell you what the company's special needs are. Some of the questions to ask are: 'If there is one thing that I could do for you in the next 30 days, what would it be?' Or 'If you could add or subtract one thing from the incumbent's (previous employee's) performance, what might that be?'

The Interview is Never Over!

Dave Theobald, President of NetShare.com in Novato, California, and former executive recruiter, says:

> Remember, the interview is never over. A 'trick' I used when I was in the search business would be to conclude the interview and suggest we have lunch, a drink, or whatever was appropriate. I could see the candidate relax and offer a sigh of relief. Then over lunch (or the drink), he would proceed to tell me things that gave me the true insight into who he really was, including things he shouldn't have said – he forgot that the interview was never over!
>
> It is also critical that you remember that if there isn't a chemistry, culture, or philosophical fit, forget it! Don't rationalize this and kid yourself into believing that you can either fix or live with whatever it is that isn't totally comfortable.

It's All About Attitude!

Peter Newfield, President of YourMissingLink.com and ResumeMachine.com in Goldens Bridge, New York, writes:

> I always tell people that interviewing is a game and the name of the game is to get a job offer. If you get an offer, then you can decide if you want to take it. If you don't get the offer, there is nothing to decide.

Go into the interview with two kinds of attitudes, regardless of what you think. One is, 'I want this job more than anything in the world and if I don't get it, I'll die'. The other is called humble egotism, which is, 'I'm great, I know I'm great, but I know I have a lot to learn'. If you go in with an attitude of show me why I should work for your company, and halfway through the interview you say to yourself, 'I'd like to work for this company,' it's too late.

9

Winning Today, Tomorrow, and in the Future

T HE YEAR 2005 IS ALMOST upon us and it's hard to believe that so much time has passed. Our parents, if still living, are getting quite elderly, our children are grown, and in fact, many of us are grandparents. We have aged gracefully (I hope!), learned many hard lessons, and become much wiser in our lives, our personal relationships, our business relationships, and our careers. The trials and tribulations of our teens and early adult years are far behind. We are more secure with who we are both personally and professionally.

I think back to my college days and the memories are still so fresh. It is difficult to believe that it has been decades since I was there. I think back to my first real job and the valuable lessons that I learned about being a professional, performing a professional task and delivering professional results. I began to understand how companies worked, what they valued in their employees, and how I could position myself for recognition and success.

That job, and every one since, have been building blocks, creating the foundation for my entire career, one that I look at with great satisfaction. Can you feel the same pride in your successes, contributions, and achievements? If you are reading this book, I would assume that your answer is yes. You've had a successful career because you've been serious about your profession and now you're serious about your job search. That seriousness, devotion, and dedication to a job well done has served you in good stead all of these years and will continue to do so in the future.

What messages did we learn from our parents about being a professional and managing our career? We learned that large corporations provide stability, professional opportunity and the potential for advancement. We learned that if we did a good job, worked hard, demonstrated professional behaviors, and delivered strong results, we would be secure. We learned that the company considered us family and would take care of their own. Most of us launched our careers believing that if we could find the right company, the right home, we would be there until retirement.

What a rude awakening many of us had! During our professional lifetimes, the world of corporate employment has changed so dramatically that all of our earlier teachings have been virtually obliterated. As thousands upon thousands of companies have laid off, downsized, rightsized, reengineered, and reinvented themselves, so have we had to reinvent ourselves, rethink our expectations, and redefine our objectives. For the 52-year-old aerospace engineer...the 47-year-old technology sales executive...the 59-year-old general manager...and hundreds of thousands of others, the professional legacy our parents left us has disintegrated before our eyes.

As a result, we have been faced with several options:

- Look for another position with a large corporation and take our chances that the next company would offer more stability.
- Transition our focus to small and mid-size companies where we believe better and more stable opportunities exist.
- Launch an entrepreneurial venture on our own or in partnership with others.
- Transfer our knowledge and experience into the consulting arena.
- Retire, take our money, and move to the beach!

If we eliminate the last item from our discussion, all of the others require that we become more educated about job search and lifelong career management. We must each take control of our own career destiny, for the most vital lesson that each of us has learned is that we cannot look to our employers for security. The sense of family that was so pervasive in our parents' generation is gone and we have had to learn that the only security in the job market is that which we create for ourselves, from ourselves. That is the reality of today's employment market.

After we have struggled to learn this lesson, it is now time to pass the lesson along to our children and our grandchildren as they embark on their careers. It is our responsibility to teach them how to manage, succeed, and prosper in today's dynamic and ever-changing employment market. And not only is it our responsibility to them, it is our responsibility to ourselves. The assumption is made that anyone reading this book is actively engaged in a job search. It is critical that as you teach these lessons, you also learn to live by them and change your beliefs, expectations, and behaviors.

My Challenge To You

My challenge to you is to design your own career and take control of your own destiny. Never again allow yourself to be placed in a position where someone else has such omnipotent influence over your professional life. Realize that you are faced with:

- **Ever increasing and tougher competition.** This is particularly true at the executive level where many individuals have comparable skills and qualifications. What will distinguish you from the crowd is your attitude and your potential fit with an organization. At your level, you must always remember that companies are not just hiring the professional, but also, and just as importantly, the person.

> *Never fear change. Change spurs growth and growth spurs positive professional performance.*

- **A greater shift toward self-employment, consulting, and interim executive positions** where a company is afforded the luxury of hiring you for a special assignment, project, or function without a long-term financial and employment commitment.

- **A greater demand for personal technology skills.** Although in the past many of your technical responsibilities may have been handled by your staff, today many of these responsibilities are now yours. Don't fall behind the curve!

- **A greater thrust on globalization.** Countries and continents once days away are now only seconds away with the emergence of the latest information and telecommunications technologies. Companies are no longer so tightly bound by geographic boundaries. And companies are taking advantage of these opportunities. We must all come to accept this change, appreciate the value of multicultural and multinational organizations, and leverage any and all international experience to our benefit.

How well you are able to respond to these changes in the workplace will dictate your career success – today and in the future. No longer can you be passive, waiting for each new opportunity to present itself to you. You must be clear about your goals and objectives, secure in your professional competencies, successful in marketing your qualifications, and proactive in managing your career. If you do not take the lead, someone else will.

Educated job seekers are winners, and winners seek new opportunities and new challenges. They have an attitude and aura of success, and are never intimidated by the unknown. They are leaders who take control and move forward, leveraging their past experiences to create new opportunities and achieve new results. These individuals will always be in demand, just as you are today.

By reading this book and devoting the time, energy, and resources to your job search that you have, you are already one of the winners. Continued success to you!

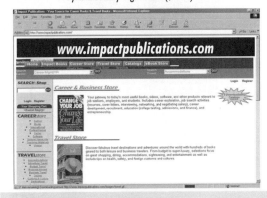